Last of the Tinsmiths

Last of the Tinsmiths

The Life of Willie MacPhee

Sheila Douglas

BIRLINN

First published in 2006 by
Birlinn Limited
West Newington House
10 Newington Road
Edinburgh
EH9 1QS

www.birlinn.co.uk

ISBN10: 1 84158 511 4
ISBN13: 978 1 84158 511 6

Briti͏ ͏ta
A cat ͏m

Printe͏ ͏ing

Contents

Preface

This book is a factual account of the life and accomplishments of the great Willie MacPhee, who lived from 1910 until 2002. He was a tradition bearer of the travelling people, who never lived in a house and did not read or write; a poor man all his days but incredibly rich in cultural terms.

It would be impossible to appreciate how true this is without including the stories he told, the songs he sang and the pipe tunes he played. Piping was the great passion of Willie's life, without his ever becoming involved in the commercial scene of which even his close relatives, the Stewarts, were a part. At the same time, he recorded his stories for me as part of my doctoral field recordings and they ended up with his songs in the Sound Archive of the School of Scottish Studies.

I had the great good fortune to have Louise Hay as one of my language students at the RSAMD's Scottish Music course. She had met Willie at a piping competition in Strathmiglo when she was fourteen years old. It was she who was able to listen to my recordings and transcribe these pipe tunes. My son Colin transcribed the music for the songs.

I am grateful to Cathie and Isaac, whose mother was Bella, but who regarded Willie as their father, and also his nephew James, for their contributions to the book. Jimmy Macgregor, a retired policeman in Perthshire, who was also a singer and entertainer, remembered Willie as always being at Traditional Music & Song Association Festivals and also at piping competitions at Aberfeldy.

Willie kept his tinsmithing stake and tools all his life, and when they were stolen from a shed beside his trailer on the Doubledykes Caravan Site, he would not let me write to the local paper about it, saying he would deal with it himself. The days of his 'good right hook' were past, but like most of his misfortunes, Willie accepted them stoically. The Last of the Tinsmiths was a truly remarkable man.

Sheila Douglas
September 2006

1 Glimpses of an Ancient Way of Life

If you keep your eyes and ears open in the Scottish countryside, even today, you can catch a glimpse of an ancient, aboriginal people, known in the eighteenth-century Highlands as the *luchd siubhail,* literally, the travelling people. Originally they were the metalworkers to the ancient clans, forced by the topography of the landscape to travel round the various glens to do their work. They made weapons and ornaments needed by the clansmen. They were also the newsbringers and the entertainers. This is why although *sorning,* staying in outbuildings without the permission of the proprietor, came to be forbidden by law, in the remoter areas of the country, this was hard to enforce. Most farmers and country-dwellers welcomed people who had been further afield and who besides could liven up the long nights with pipes and stories. These were the family groups who moved about, working as a team to ply their ancient craft and keep on good terms with the smallholders and people of the glens. Historical change has repeatedly robbed them of their livelihood; they have survived by their own strength of character, ingenuity and quick-wittedness. I really understand what John Stewart, the younger brother of Alec, who was included in my *King o the Black Art* project, described as 'being traveller-brained', but too many people think of them as backward drop-outs, liars and thieves. How wrong these people were and how wrong they still are cannot be shown in any better way than describing the life of a man like Willie MacPhee.

Of course, as I discovered early on, there is a difference between the attitudes of 'townies' and country people to travellers. The former are far less tolerant and lack understanding of their way of life, and the latter are usually the opposite. The farming community depended on travellers for seasonal work and also for providing useful articles like tinware, baskets and heather besoms. A local farmer, who was also a regional councillor, once visited me to 'put me right about the travellers'. But he made a distinction between what he called 'oor traivellers', whose work he valued, whose names he knew and for whose welfare he was concerned, and those who came from elsewhere. Betsy Whyte confirmed to me that this was typical of Perthshire farmers, who had the same travellers working for them year after year. Duncan Campbell of Glenlyon in his memoirs in 1910 spoke kindly of the travellers who came to work seasonally on his father's small farm and those of his neighbours. One of them, who he knew as Donald Ruadh, used to give him a ride on his cuddy, a great thrill for a wee lad. The travellers were allowed to camp in the farm kiln, where they worked at tinsmithing and, in the time of Duncan Campbell's grandfather, pre-1746, even silversmithing. A lad called Elijah they accepted in to their family circle, and he was brought up by Duncan's grandmother; he was related to Willie MacPhee's cousins, the Stewarts.

Nowadays of course many travellers live in houses and are hard to distinguish from the rest of the community. Yet although many of them have left the travelling life behind them, you can still stumble on sights and sounds that seem to belong to the past round any corner in the glens and straths, or even in the city streets of present-day Scotland. Perhaps you might see a lived-in trailer drawn away from the road onto a patch of land by a burn, sheltered by bracken, gorse and heather. Or maybe you will spot a broad-shouldered figure with a weathered face and work-calloused hands driving a car or lorry loaded with scrap between hawthorn hedges. Or, in towns, you might hear quick high voices exchanging light-hearted banter over a can of beer in an alleyway or over drams in a corner of a pub. You may see a tartan-clad piper by the roadside in the Highlands, catering for the romantic dreams of the tourists. Certainly Willie MacPhee and his cousin Alec Stewart did this in Glencoe and up by Loch Lochy for years.

You may pass by without noticing or even giving them a thought, but they are surviving remnants of a very ancient way of life: a remnant that has preserved not only the precious traditions of kinship and hospitality that are central to Scottish culture, but also the stories and songs that our schools, political system, social snobbery and the media have caused us almost to forget. In the Folk Revival of the 1960s and 1970s the singers, musicians and storytellers among the surviving travellers became famous and influential as sources of the old, neglected traditions. These included Belle and Alec Stewart, their daughters, Cathie and Sheila, their cousin, Jeannie Robertson, her daughter, Lizzie Higgins, her nephew Stanley and his sister Janet, Betsy Whyte and Duncan Williamson. Willie MacPhee became well known and well loved and was always there, but did not become part of what was to become the commercial scene. Over the centuries generations of travellers have kept alive story versions and songs and ballads in oral tradition. That means they had never seen them in print till crazy people like the late, great Hamish Henderson, the co-founder of the School of Scottish Studies and driving force of the Folk Revival, to whose attention the Stewarts were brought by Maurice Fleming, and others, including myself, not only recorded them but also lived with them and learned from them. Their understanding of the value and wisdom that these stories and songs hold is understood fully only when you see them in the context of lives of poverty and hardship. And these harsh conditions really bring out the inner strength, adaptability and resourcefulness of these remarkable folk, with minimal schooling but a strong sense of what is important in life.

I have had the privilege of enjoying the friendship of a number of the travelling people for over forty years, including Willie and Bella MacPhee. Willie was the first cousin of Alec Stewart of Blairgowrie, whose family's stories I recorded between 1979 and 1985. I included Willie's stories in the project and subsequent story collection, *The King o the Black Art*, published by Aberdeen University Press in 1987. For years, Alec and Willie were more like brothers, sharing a love of piping, storytelling and ceilidhing generally. Alec's family were unusual among settled travellers in that they did not leave their traditions behind them, but kept them alive, at least among the older generation. Of course, these traditions proved to be a fruitful source of making a living, but they also brought more and better recognition of the travelling way of life and heritage of song, tune and story. Alec died in 1980, aged seventy-six, of leukaemia, and Belle passed on in 1997 at the age of ninety-one. Willie, who never lived in a house, was born in 1910 and lasted until 2002; he now lies at rest in Gartocharn, within sight of Loch Lomond, a fitting resting-place for a man who loved the beauty of the landscape. Bella was alive until recently, but afflicted by age's cruel habit of confusing the mind and destroying the memory. My son Colin and I attended her funeral in Perth. She had been cared for in her declining years by a devoted daughter Cathie and granddaughter Bella. Cathie's brother Isaac and his family lived near at hand in Perth and were always present to help with any problems. To them all I owe a great debt of gratitude for sharing with me the riches of their traditions. In my graveside tribute to Belle Stewart in 1997, I thanked her and all the travelling people for reminding us of our ancient values, songs and stories. I would certainly extend that tribute to include Willie and Bella.

The travellers had to find other ways of getting by besides making weapons and ornaments, and they turned to making more useful articles like baskets and doing seasonal farm work in order to survive. Willie MacPhee was the latest generation of a people who have always been enabled by their incredible resourcefulness and versatility to turn their hands to some other way of making a living. The making of silver brooches, clasps, buckles and daggers to go with Highland dress that was proscribed by law after the Jacobite rising of 1745 was replaced by tinsmithing and the mending of pots, pans and kettles. Horse-trading became car dealing; seasonal farm-work at the neeps, tatties and berries went along with besom and basket-making and the fashioning of hornware to support the country folk.

Song, story and music on pipes, fiddles and accordions played an important part in their lives and many of them were highly talented, like Alec and John's father, Jock, who married Willie's paternal aunt Nancy. He became one of the best pipers in Scotland, winning gold medals at the Games and becoming a member of the Atholl Highlanders. He appears in a photograph of a group of the leading pipers taken at the Atholl Gathering at the beginning of the twentieth century. The Stewarts of Blair are world famous and both Alec and John became notable pipers in their turn. John's son Alec, better known as Toby, became a successful accordionist on the variety stage. Willie's mother, Maggie Cameron, featured as a storyteller in the *Radio Ballad* on the travellers made by Charles Parker and Ewan MacColl in the 1950s. Charles Parker was the pioneer of 'actuality radio' in which he used taped voices without a narrator, juxtaposing settled people's views on travellers and travellers' accounts of how 'the hantle' had treated them, so as to emphasise the lack of understanding between them. Ewan MacColl was a singer/songwriter who wrote songs for the programmes. The queen awarded Belle the BEM in 1986 for her services to folk music.

The urban folk revivalists of the 1960s found the travellers had kept alive much of the Scots tradition and in some areas were almost the only sources of it. The settled population had become too educated and media-influenced either to value it or to practise it. A huge debt is owed to the travellers for this alone. It is also a powerful proof of their Scottish identity. As already noted, many of them are settled in houses. Some of the more prosperous and pretentious among them are ready to deny their traveller origins. The younger generations of their families go to school and, nowadays, to university, watch television and DVDs, and mostly reject their grandparents' traditional songs and stories.

An American student, Michael Campbell from Seattle, came over on a scholarship in the early 1990s and did a project on traveller storytellers, for which he recorded Belle Stewart, Willie MacPhee, Stanley Robertson and his sister Janet, and Duncan Williamson; he also interviewed their children and other younger relatives. They confirmed that they were not interested in such things, but that they knew they meant a lot to their parents and grandparents. Some thought they might come back to them when they were older. Those who still travel have to contend with laws designed to force them, if not off the road, at least onto council-run caravan sites or into council houses from which they can send their children to school. It's a benign form of assimilation, but it *is* assimilation.

There are now comparatively few staying on the road and out of houses and retaining their old skills and trades. Willie MacPhee was one of the last survivors of this group. The nearest he came to living in a house was being given a stance on Doubledykes caravan site at Inveralmond on the outskirts of Perth, set up by Perth and Kinross Council in accordance with government policy. The local authority never acknowledged the huge contribution the travellers had made to the community, but instead always regarded it as a privilege for travellers to benefit from being allowed to stop on sites and send their children to local schools. A questionnaire I gave to a former maths teacher at Blairgowrie High School about his experience of traveller children in the school failed to elicit any positive response to enquiries about the culture and traditions the travellers had. This was a man well disposed to travellers and interested in their welfare, but he did not think of asking them. People are beginning to waken up to the ways in which travellers contribute to society, but there is still a good bit to go. Perhaps this book will help to foster the idea that it is possible to be a traveller and also a great Scottish tradition bearer. The fact that nowadays the Folk Revival of the 1960s and 1970s has been airbrushed out of Scotland's musical history cannot overlook people like Willie MacPhee, who was never part of the commercial scene.

To the question of the origin of the Scottish travellers there is no simple answer, and there is no hard and fast historical evidence to prove any of the various theories that have been put forward. Calum MacLean, co-founder of the School of Scottish Studies, described them as 'descendants of itinerant craftsmen' and Hamish Henderson and Tim Neat, maker of the film of *The Summer Walkers* and already engaged in writing a biography of

Hamish, saw 'a link between traveller tinsmiths and the great metalworkers of Celtic society in the Heroic Age'. The Romans never really conquered the Highlands, so age-old ways continued there outside the influence of classical civilisation, as they did in most of the Scottish islands. Ross Noble, who was curator of the Kingussie Folk Museum, pointed out that the travellers' name in Gaelic describes their function: 'They were known in Gaelic as *cairdean*, the ironworkers or metalworkers, and their original function was to go round from warring clan to warring clan, making weapons and repairing weapons; they were the armourers of these warrior Celtic princes. Many of the travellers themselves believed that their forebears were the remnants of the scattered clans after Culloden, although their skills are much older than that. The clans themselves have an equally shadowy history and 'claim legendary progenitors with whom their connection is based simply on oral tradition and for which there is no proof.' Of course, oral tradition is not an entirely unreliable source of information, as William Motherwell, one of the most important of the early nineteenth-century song collectors made a point of saying in the introduction to his *Minstrelsy of the Scottish Borders* (Paisley, 1828):

> The tear and wear of three centuries will do less mischief to the text of an old ballad among the vulgar, than one short hour will effect, if in the possession of some sprightly and accomplished editor of the present day who may choose to impose on himself the thankless and uncalled for labour of piecing and patching up its imperfections, polishing its asperities, correcting its mistakes, embellishing its naked details, purging it of impurities, and of trimming it from top to toe with tailor-like fastidiousness and nicety, so as to be made fit for the press.

What set Motherwell on this road was the advice of Sir Walter Scott, to whom he had sent a collated version of a ballad for his approval. Having himself collated many versions in his *Minstrelsy*, Scott confessed to him in a letter, 'In fact, I think I did wrong myself in endeavouring to make the best possible set of an ancient ballad out of several copies obtained from different quarters, and that in many respects, if I improved the poetry, I spoiled the simplicity of the old song.' This is what made Motherwell the first modern song collector: he took Scott's advice, and thereafter respected the material he got from singers like Agnes Lyle and others in the Kilbarchan weaving community. Scott had been doing only what literary-minded song collectors had been doing before him, none of them realising that what is composed to be sung is not the same thing as what is written to be read. In other words, song lyrics and ballads are not poetry and obey different rules. It is thrilling to see the ability of people like Willie, who do not learn songs out of books but by hearing them, just as they learn oral tales and pipe tunes. Listening to such a person is a revelation, because it shows someone who is not making use of material for his own ends, but because he loves it and it is a part of him. Belle Stewart once said to me, 'There are two kinds of singer: one who says, "Listen to this bonnie song", and the other who says, "Listen to *me* singing this bonnie song." Willie was undoubtedly the former, and the same goes for his storytelling and his piping. He looked on himself as part of something that had come from the past and would continue into the future, what Hamish Henderson described as 'the carrying stream'.

The travelling people are sometimes referred to by uninformed urban folk as gypsies, but one thing is certain: they are not the same. The gypsies certainly came to Britain from Europe in the sixteenth century, as *Northern Chronicle* editor, Duncan

Campbell of Glenlyon, pointed out in his memoirs, 'to put upon James V' who passed favourable laws to protect them. They reached the Borders, but tended not to advance very much further north, although there may have been intermarriage with both travelling and settled Scots from the sixteenth century onward. That they did not move north of the Borders in any great numbers is almost certainly because they found native metalworkers there already, as happened in Ireland. In fact there seems to be some similarity between the origins of the Scottish and Irish travellers, as Sharon Gmelch points out in *To Shorten The Road*: 'Not all the travelling people originated at the same time. Some families have been on the road for centuries, while others have become itinerant in recent times. Moreover they did not all originate in the same way. First, tradesmen and specialists often became itinerant because the population in their area changed and consequently the demand for their skills was not great enough to allow them to remain sedentary. Secondly, many peasants were forced onto the road through evictions, unemployment and famine. Thirdly, there have always been drop-outs from settled society – persons who left their homes due to some personal misfortune or indiscretion or who simply chose to live an itinerant life.'

Scottish travellers are made up of the same elements, in which only the oldest sort were tinsmiths or tinkers. Those who are dropouts can be easily distinguished from the rest for they are loners, while tinkers travel or live in family groups, which are very important to them. Sharon Gmelch goes on to describe how in early Christian times 'itinerant whitesmiths, working in bronze, gold and silver, travelled the countryside, making personal ornaments, weapons and horse-trappings, in return for food and lodging'. This matches the account of Duncan Campbell of Glenlyon, a teacher and journalist, born in 1828, who wrote of tinkers in the time of his grandfather as 'skilled silversmiths' who 'made brooches, rings and clasps for girdles or to decorate the hilts of swords and daggers' (*Reminiscences and Reflections of an Octogenarian Highlander,* Inverness 1910). The fact that Gmelch was writing about the tenth century and Campbell was writing about the eighteenth century serves only to indicate the antiquity of the metalworking tradition, whose secrets had been handed down through countless generations. Since they were skilled at melting down metal objects in order to create new ones, many people held them in superstitious awe. This was what earned the tinkers their reputation as workers of magic.

Historical change has repeatedly rendered obsolete the ancient skills of the travellers through changing fashion, technological progress and political and social upheaval, such as when the Act of Proscription of 1746 forbade the wearing of Highland dress and the carrying of weapons. As Duncan Campbell wrote succinctly in his memoirs, 'when the demand ceased, the art was soon lost'. The resourceful metalworkers then resorted to the making of more useful articles of tinware, such as kettles, bowls, flagons, pans and strainers, as well as horn spoons, baskets, besoms and scrubbers, all needed by the 'country hantle' in the fertile straths, where farmlands also provided seasonal work. The farming community and the travellers were to some extent interdependent. The idea that dispossessed people after the Jacobite Rising or during the Clearances that followed (euphemistically described as 'improvements' by some Highland landowners) could have taken up the occupations of the traveller is demonstrably absurd: why should the dispossessed clansmen find it useful to learn trades that the travellers have had to give up because they were forbidden by law? In other words, the travelling people themselves had to change their trades, because the old ones had become out of date.

I have come to admire the travellers for their social skills, knowing what to say when and where and how to please people. This ability to articulate in what teachers would call 'the right register' has been one of the means used by them to survive, and they are very skilled in it, without the people they are manipulating being aware of what is going on. This is very much a difficulty for the collector, because if you ask them questions, they will give you the answer you want, whether it is true or not. The secret is not to ask loaded questions, but start off with something general like 'Where were you born?' or 'Do you know that part of the country?' or 'Do you have a story/song/ballad for me tonight?' Then you should just let them talk about whatever they want, tell whatever story or sing whatever song they want and save any questions for another time. I must say, Willie MacPhee was exceptional as far as I was concerned because he was always truthful and open; I could really trust what he said, and many times was proved right to do so. His storytelling and singing and piping were always enjoyable and enthralling. He also did not share the influences that caused Alec's family, the Stewarts of Blair, to paint themselves as tragic romantic 'pilgrims of the mist' with their own 'language' and a history of persecution. Folklorists with a political agenda have encouraged them to claim that Cant is their 'language' and therefore part of their identity.

The Perthshire Cant includes the following words or groups of words. This phonetically spelled list was compiled by me from the words Belle Stewart told me about.

Glossary of Perthshire Cant

anee: in, back

avree: away

bammins: clutter, mess

barracade: large tent, with stove and chimney

barrie: good

beerie: boat

bene: good (French *bien*, Scots *bien*)

bene patren: minister

bene patren's ken: church

bene yerram: blood

beneship davies: good day

bing: come, go

bing avree: go away

blaswag: bag

blinkum: match

bow-tent: tent made from cloth-covered bent hazel boughs

brickets: trousers

broskin: car

buffert: dog

carnis: meat (Latin *carnis*)

chate: thing

chatterie: goods, stuff

chore: steal

chourie: knife (Romany)

cluishes: ears (from Gaelic)

coull: man

country hantle: settled people

deek: look, see

dilly: girl, young woman

dodder: doctor

doomie: back

drom: road (Romany)

drookerin: reading palms, telling fortunes

faizen: hair

feek: give

femmels: fingers, hand

fichles: rags

flattrin: fish

gadgie: man (derogatory)

gannie: hen

geddie: boy, young man

gellie: a bow-tent (Scots word for a bothy)

glimmer: fire

granyie: ring

granzie: barn

grenum: corn, grain

grib: take, hold

gruffie: pig (*guffie* is a Scots word for fat)

gry: horse (Romany)

haben: food

hand chates: cigarettes

hornie feekie: policeman

jan: know, understand

jeer: excrement

jurival: genitals

keer: house
kain: house
kinchin: child
kip: bed
lour: money
magelum: potato
mang: speak
manishee: woman (Romany)
mazie: cup (Scots *mazer*)
mazies: dishes
megget: sheep
moich: fool
monticleer: water
mookie: kiss
moolie: kill (from Scots *mools* for earth)
morricans: belly, body
mort: woman (Perthshire)
mush-feeker: umbrella mender
mutyie: rabbit
naiscoull: father
naiscoull coull: priest
naismort: mother
naken: traveller
pannie: water (Romany)
peeve: drink
peevin kain: pub
pennam: bread (from Latin *panis*)
persteejie: cart, coach
pluffer: pipe
pooskie coull: gamekeeper
poris: pocket

rowtler: cow (*rowt* is Scots word for bellow)
ruffie: devil
scaldie: a person who lives in a house and works at a job
shan: bad (from Gaelic *sean*)
shannas: badness
snottam: hook for hanging pot over fire
sprach: beg (from German *sprechen*, *sprach*, to speak)
stall: stop
stardie: prison
strammel: straw
stumers: bagpipes
stumerer coull: piper
sweetnie: sugar
test: head
tramplers: feet
trash: afraid
tuggerie: clothes
tullum: spoon
vile: town (French *ville*, Gaelic *baile*)
wanner: buy, sell
weed: tea
whammlin cacavie: a boiling kettle (Scots *whammle*: bubbling or boiling)
winklers: eyes
yarra: eggs
yerram: milk

Willie's observations on the Cant language are interesting and revealing. Like any private language, Cant is for many travellers a distinctive mark of identity. It may have been at one time a more fully developed language with grammar and syntax than is spoken today even among older travellers. But that time has long ago been lost sight of, and with characteristic common sense Willie declared that its use nowadays, in dealing with police and local authority officials, was 'counter-productive'. Pragmatically he realised that the need for Cant had lessened considerably and, while he was a traditionalist, he was unlikely to argue that a thing must go on being done because it has 'aye been'. Besides, no one could possibly believe that a man, even a man who could not read and write, who had enough command of words to be able to use such a term as 'counter-productive', could possibly be satisfied to use a language as limited as Cant. It was originally a means by which travellers concealed the meaning of what was said, particularly in the presence of non-travellers, when doing deals. Willie was very definite about the fact that travellers never used to speak Cant among themselves; in fact he denied this seven times. Two other things have to be pointed out. The incidence of Romany words is an indicator of how the Scottish travellers have mixed with gypsies, both in the Borders and further south. Their similar lifestyles have meant that they have found themselves pursuing the same seasonal or casual work in hop, and other harvest, fields, and on building sites. One branch of the Stewart family, for example, has intermarried with English gypsies, called Hilton, encountered on trips to the south of England for seasonal work.

Secondly, the Cant used by the Perthshire travellers varies from that used by the Aberdeen ones. For example, tea is *weed* in Perthshire but *slab* in Aberdeenshire; money is *lour* in Perthshire, but *lowie* or *lowdie* in Aberdeenshire. A pig is a *gruffie* in Perthshire and a *guffie* in Aberdeenshire. Eyes are *winklers* in Perthshire but *yaks* in Aberdeenshire. A fool is a *moich* in Perthshire, but a *corach* in Aberdeenshire. The term *naken* for a traveller in Perthshire is rendered as *nyakim* by Aberdeenshire Stanley Robertson in the title of his book *Nyakim's Windows*. Actually, *naken* means 'self'.

Sheila Stewart told me recently that her grandmother told her that words like *gadgie* and *barra* are what she called 'slang Cant' used to help keep the true Cant a secret. The real Cant, to her, was *coull* and *bene*. Hamish Henderson said that he was told that *gadgie* was used of a man, meaning one other than a traveller man. All word use can change with time and place, and Cant is no exception. Cant has the ability to form new name words as required by using the all-purpose word *chate* (thing): *miaowin chate* (cat), *whuddin chate* (radio), *lowpin chate* (frog), *nab chate* (hankie), *stallin chate* (chair), *glimmer chate* (match), *bavver chate* (needle) and *lour chate* (valuable or piece of jewellery). Other words can be made by using *gadgie* or *coull* in the same way: *sprachin gadgie* (beggar), *carnis gadgie* (butcher), *stumerer coull* (piper) and *strod coull* (shoemaker).

There is also a Gaelic-based Cant used in the far north of Scotland by travelling people. This is called Beurla Regaird, or the language of the metalworker as Calum MacLean translated it, which hints at an ancient origin, and is akin to the Beurla gun Seur (guessed spelling) in Ireland. There are also Gaelic words or words with possible Gaelic connections in Perthshire Cant, including: *cluishes* (ears), *shan* (bad, from *sean*), *fichles* (rags, from *fughell*), and *snottam* (pothook). As Morag MacLeod of the School of Scottish Studies has pointed out, Willie MacPhee also uses a word *gourach* for the fork of a tree, which corresponds to the Gaelic word for a fork or crotch. In Ewan MacColl's book on the Stewarts, *Till Doomsday in the Afternoon*, he includes in his list of Cant the words *cailleach*, which is Gaelic for an old woman, *ruadh*, which is Gaelic for red and *clach*, which is Gaelic for a stone. There are three words in Beurla Regaird which correspond to words in Perthshire Cant: *fidileas* (*fichles*, rags), *caineag* (*gannie*, hen) and *cain* (*kain*, house). Since the latter also relates to the Elizabethan slang word 'ken', also meaning house, that Hamish Henderson found in *The Caveat for Common Cursitors*, a handbook of Elizabethan thieves' slang written by Thomas Harman in the sixteenth century, one can only speculate on how it came about or in which direction it spread.

There are also old Scots words still used by travellers, who think they are Cant because they are no longer commonly used by the settled people. These include: *lerrick* (larch tree), *mowdit* (buried), *hantle* (part or piece), *siskin* (a type of bird), *mools* (earth), *mazer* (wooden) cup, *gellie* (a bothy), *rowt* (bellow), *rowtler* (cow), *screeve* (write), *speugie* (sparrow), and *coories* (blankets: to 'coorie' is to crouch down or curl up, as you do in bed).

Although its usage may be less nowadays, Cant still lives on the memories of older travellers, even settled ones. There are no abstract words in Cant or even words that relate to abstract ideas unless *barrie* or *bene* and *shan* for good and bad might count. The sons and daughters and grandchildren of older travellers do not find the need to use Cant in the present day, unless for humorous or nostalgic purposes. It was never a complete language in itself, but the use of it in relation to trade contributed to the sense, both amongst travellers themselves, and among settled folk, of a separate caste within society. At one time it would have attracted no attention as many social groups had their own terminology. And of course there never has been a time in our history when we have used only one language in Scotland, a fact that is often forgotten in the tendency to think of Scots as 'just a form of English', which it is not. As with most other things, travellers used whatever was helpful to them at the time, then later discarded it when it was no longer needed. This seems to have been what motivated Willie MacPhee's use of Cant.

It is in the oral culture of the travellers – the songs, music and stories, riddles and proverbs, beliefs and customs, handed down through many generations like their metalworking skills – that one finds the most convincing proof of their identity. 'They still keep alive an ancient and vital oral literature that makes theirs one of the most dynamic folk cultures of Europe', as Timothy Neat, author of *The Summer Walkers,* based on his film of that name, believed. In his work he also demonstrated that, 'they are carriers of an essentially Celtic culture'. Along with this literature, the musical traditions of bagpiping and singing were notable among certain travelling families, including the Stewarts. Willie MacPhee was closely related to them, being a full first cousin to Alec Stewart. His story repertoire was different from theirs, partly because some of it was handed down in *his* family, and partly because his early travelling, as well as crossing their path, took him along different routes and by different camping grounds than theirs. The MacPhees were a huge clan found all over the west of Scotland. The Perthshire Stewarts, within recent generations at least, were croft-based rather than tented like the family of the late Betsy Whyte or the Glenlyon Mackenzies were. Stewarts are also found in Aberdeenshire and Inverness-shire, as well as in Sutherland, where they are Gaelic speakers. Betsy Whyte, née Townsley, wrote of her childhood as a Perthshire tented traveller in her much-loved book *The Yellow on the Broom*. The Mackenzies are two brothers and a sister who remained tent-dwellers until fairly recently.

All his life Willie loved to ceilidh with his family and friends and retained in his memory all the stories he had learned around the campfire or in tent or trailer, however complicated they were. He learned by listening and, not only did he develop his own way of telling them, always intimate and entertaining, he understood their inner meaning, not by analysing them as a scholar might, but by some inborn intuitive wisdom that he inherited from the past. It is because of families like Willie's and Alec's that the Scottish Folk Revival was so exciting. The young urban revivalists listened to Jeannie Robertson and Belle Stewart, who became internationally famous star performers, honoured by the Queen for services to folk music. But there were others, like Willie, who attended many clubs and festivals, but shunned the limelight, never competed, and sang and told stories and played the pipes in ceilidhs and sessions. Yet there was such charisma about Willie that he became well known across the whole country. Despite the recognition, he was just doing what all his forebears had done round the fireside.

The lifestyle of the Scottish travellers echoes some of the oldest customs and beliefs of Highland society. The great value attached to family life and kinship, the importance of social life and hospitality, which includes liberal dispensing of food and drink; a general belief in the supernatural and a love of stories, songs and beautiful artefacts are all typical of the Celtic way of life. Even some of the stories I have recorded in Scots from Willie and the Stewarts have parallels in Gaelic which are closer to them any other European versions are. Willie occasionally uses words like *gourach* (a crotch in a tree) and *ceann mor* (literally 'big head', a skull) and idioms like 'who came in but So and So', 'that's my word to you,' and 'the door was a long while of being opened'. The ancestral tellers of these stories must surely have been Gaelic speaking, with a line stretching back into prehistory to forebears who spoke who knows what language. There is a lot we do not know for certain, from before the age of the tape recorder. What we do know is that the stories that were passed down have a place on the European, if not the world map of story tradition.

Willie McPhee provided a link between the ancient history of his people and their situation in present-day Scotland, for he experienced a good representative selection of the changes that affected their lives, changes which they were able to survive because of the very qualities Willie exemplified in his long life. He saw the change from horse-coping to second-hand car dealing. When he became a good mechanic in his young days he was in step with the trend of the time, not an anachronism. He had been used to travelling in horse-drawn carts or yokes and living in tents, which became living in trailers and driving cars and lorries. Many people came to know him as a magician with car engines. If he broke down, he could get the vehicle going again with a piece of bent wire. He nursed an old caravanette for seventeen years and then sold it to a storyteller friend called Paraig MacNeil. I had to travel down to Ayrshire with Paraig and, as he lives not too far from me, he promised to take me down in the old van. We broke down on the motorway and Paraig had not a clue what to do. He had to phone a friend to tow us off and we had to postpone the trip. If Willie had been there, he would have got it going! Willie MacPhee also knew what it was to be constantly moved on and fined for illegal camping by laws that made him a criminal for following his traditional way of life. This situation was improved when a farmer at Redgorton, near Perth, began to allow Willie to put his caravan into a quarry on the farm after the farm-work was finished for the day; Willie had alerted him to the fact that someone was breaking into and stealing from his outbuildings. Then he found himself living on a caravan site put up by the local council in accordance with the government's policy of non-harassment of travellers. He went from hard times, from grafting hard for every penny earned and improvising those things he could not afford to buy, to being helped to subsist by the Welfare State.

Meeting him, I soon became aware of all this history and saw him, *sub specie aeternitatis* (in a perspective that takes in eternity, or all time and space), as an archetypal human being. In this he was remarkable, a walking paradox in contemporary society's terms. He owned very little, yet was rich in traditional culture, music, song and piping. He was a man who never learned to read and write (although he taught himself to read bagpipe music) yet he was intelligent, articulate and imaginative, with an interest in contemporary events. He had never lived in a house but seemed to 'own the world's room'. His humanity made him like all of us, yet he was unique in his personal charisma and talents. His long life made him a child of the early 1900s, the age of the horse, the campfire and the seasonal crop cycle, yet because of his innate adaptability he was able to survive through the twentieth century, with its motorcars, electricity and scientific progress, into the twenty-first century. He kept alive the wisdom of the past, the importance of the humanity, sense of kinship and standards of hospitality that make our lives civilised. He shared the travellers' love of nature and the countryside, good music and stories, laughter and conviviality. He enjoyed all kinds of music and singing, even of people 'who sang in a different way' than he did. By that he meant with guitar or other instrumental accompaniment, for Willie sang unaccompanied in a high lyrical voice that was intensely passionate and expressive. He was also aware of a wider, supernaturally magical world all round him and was always interested in what was going on in it. Andrew, my late husband, who was also a close friend of Willie's, and I were often struck by the perspicacity of his comments on current affairs and his ability to see through the spin of politicians.

As a local 'English' teacher at Perth Academy, I always kept my eyes skinned for any signs of travellers among the pupils being harassed, but I never found any, either because would-be bullies were deterred by me, or because they were fully aware who their classmates were and were quite accepting of them. I certainly always made the point of explaining my traveller friends to the other pupils and used storytelling as a teaching resource, telling story versions I had learned from people like Willie. Some of the traveller pupils either knew the storytellers, or were actually related to them. I once rocked a small traveller boy back on his heels in a class I was supervising by using the Cant word '*Shannas!*' to him about his behaviour. He stopped in mid-caper and ever after looked at me with something approaching awe. I never explained how I came to know such a word. Members of staff, however, showed signs of misunderstanding: I remember having to explain to colleagues how a traveller family worked as a team. If they had to go to Aberdeen to receive goods brought by sea they kept their children off school, not just because they could not and would not leave them on their own but because they all had work to do. My colleagues also thought it very strange that Willie, who could not read and write because family circumstances had prevented him from having any schooling, should go with Bella to Perth Theatre and see a play. 'Is it not a long time for them to sit and listen?' they asked, unaware that Willie had spent so much time listening in his life that he could not only take in all kinds of things, but would remember them all afterwards. One of his stories can last an hour and a half. A few months, or a few years later he can remember the story, not word for word, but in the same sequence, even tailoring it to fit the time available and the audience. As a teacher, my eyes were opened to the fact that 'illiterate' does not necessarily mean 'stupid'.

One of Willie's best personal qualities that made him stand out as exceptional was the fact that he never said derogatory things about other travellers, or anyone else for that matter. He could see through most human foibles, but, being aware of his own humanity, he could always see some good in others, and if anyone was doing him wrong he only voiced his inability to understand why they should do such things. Cathy, Willie's stepdaughter, remembers him shaking his head and making a dismissive gesture if anyone spoke about the ill-treatment he had received. He was basically a friendly person who wanted to avoid trouble and be on good terms with others. There are other travellers like him, including his own family, but they are often afraid or do not always handle situations as well as he had learned to do. Of course, the result was that some other travellers, jealous of his skill and accomplishments, would always try to push him into the background and talk him down, but he never rose to their bait. As my late husband used to say, Willie was 'a big man in every way', who disdained to lower himself. He towered over them all and impressed other people, although he did not need to push himself forward to do so. There are, of course, other travellers who are more aggressive and unfortunately more vocal in their demands. They ask that the settled population should not only not harass them (which should be a right in any civilised society) but should treat them as special cases and allow them to do what they like, such as camping wherever they choose or getting benefits from the local council, whether or not they pay rates and taxes. No one knew better than Willie that ideas such as these cannot work: they antagonise the settled community and undermine their picture of the travellers more than anything. Willie was always courteous and co-operative when dealing with officialdom, and as a result he was treated in the same way. He and his family had no complaints about the way the Doubledykes caravan site at Inveralmond on the northern outskirts of Perth was run. The local housing department supported him when he lost his caravan in the floods, and when

I accompanied him on one visit the local official addressed him politely and even warmly. I did not speak at all so the officials had no idea I was not a traveller.

This side of Willie's character was noticed by retired police sergeant Jimmy Macgregor. His memories of him are both affectionate and respectful, both as a law-abiding man and as a piper. In fact, it would be hard to find anyone who knew him who has a hard word to say about him.

Willie had a sense of humour too, which meant he was good company. He did not mind letting people think his first-person way of storytelling was not just a choice of technique to add impact, but a truly autobiographical touch. Even a seasoned storyteller could be taken in on first acquaintance, like Helen East, a well-known London-based storyteller whose hospitality Willie enjoyed when he first went down south with Duncan Williamson. By contrast, most listeners in Scotland would chuckle when he said, 'When I was a young man, I couldnae dae onythin. I couldnae play the pipes or sing or tell a story.' It was part of the fun for him to say things listeners knew could not be true. He would keep his face straight and admonish them with, 'Dinna you laugh! It could happen to to you as it's happened to me!' He liked humorous songs, both Scottish and Irish, and sang them with gusto, especially about drinking and courting. His great love was piping, and he was especially popular with tourists of all nationalities because he would play any tune they asked for and remain good-humoured. Isaac, Willie's stepson, says Willie always maintained his pipes very well, so that they would always play well. Louise Hay, transcriber of his tunes and teacher of piping in Inverness schools and a long-time friend of Willie and Bella, noticed this. The actors in the first stage production of *The Yellow on the Broom*, adapted by Anne Downie, from Betsy Whyte's book, were thrilled to meet him and Bella in the Adam

Smith Theatre in Kirkcaldy. I went with them to see the play there and it opened with the actor playing Betsy's father singing my 'Willie MacPhee's Song' at a campfire. To meet the man himself was something they obviously enjoyed and they were clearly very impressed by him.

Before I start telling Willie's story and seeing how it is bound up with the stories he told, I must consider why he was such a great storyteller. The travellers have always had many uses for storytelling and valued stories among themselves for many reasons. It is easy to recognise how they used stories to pass on wisdom, strengthen family and community ties and help people to cope with life's problems. They have even been known, as Willie's cousin John Stewart told me, to deal and swap stories, using them as currency to pay for something. Stories were above anything else entertaining, and had to be, for, as more than one traveller has put it to me, 'These stories were our education.' A good example of this is 'The Three Feathers', a story version told by Willie and also by the Stewarts.

The Three Feathers

There was once a king and he had three sons. Now he wasnae a very rich king, jist aboot a moderate man, as ye'd say, ye ken. And he waukened up this mornin an haed a luik roon his place an he didnae see very much value in onythin he had, ye know. So he thocht til himsel, 'Now I cannae live that long masel, I'm getting very auld and I dinnae ken what I can dae for these boys o mine. If I divide this castle up in wee bits, they'll hae nothin!' Ye see. So he thocht this wee plan up and got his three boys thegither an he says, 'Look, boys,' he says, 'I'm gaun tae be fair wi ye,' he says. 'There's no much in this castle ye can see,' he says. 'We've selt everythin we had tae get some money and

there's no much money in the kitty,' he says. 'So I'll tell ye whit
we're gaun tae dae,' he says. 'I know ma time is aboot up, saw
I'm gauntae gie yeze aa a wee task tae dae an the one that did the
best task,' he says, 'I'll gie him the castle an the ither twa can gae
off an dae their best for them self.'

So they quite agreed tae that, ye see.

'Well,' the auldest son says, 'whit's the task, faither?'

He says, 'I want yeze tae go away, different directions and
bring me back a rug, 'he says,' a bedspread rug for the top o the
bed,' he says, 'and whoever brings the best one back, he's the
one who'll get the castle,' he says.

So they went up to the battlements at the top o the castle and
they each took oot a goose feather. The auldest brither took his
goose feather an threw it up in the air and whichever direction it
fell on the thick end, wis the direction he had to take. And off
he went to the north. The second brither took his feather and
threw it up and it circled aboot for a bit then fell tae the sooth
and off he went. Noo the youngest brither wis supposed tae be a
wee bit dopey, he wisnae quite aa there upstairs, and the way
he threw up his feather, he must have thrown it up too hard and
it went up owre the waa, and went awa doon the back o the
castle.

Sae the twa aulder brithers gaed off and they were awa a lang
time, and of course the daftie cam oot and went doon roon the
back o the castle tae luik for where his feather haed landed. And
he was huntin through aa these weeds and nettles and grass
which hadnae been cut for years and years. And he's luikin
everywhere for this feather and he comes upon this big stone
and there wis a ring on it and on top of the stone wis his feather.
And he didnae pey ony heed tae which wey it wis pointin, he
jist picked it up. And he looked at this stone, a big square stone
with a big ring on it and he thought it was a well or something.

He lifted it and edged it up a wee bit and he looked doon and he saw some steps leading down intae this hole in the grun.

'Oh,' he says, 'there's steps gaun doon,' he says. Sae he decides tae follow these steps and goes doon about thirty or forty feet under the ground, and when he come tae the bottom, there was a great big long passage, like a mine, going away far under the ground. It wasnae like an ordinary passage in a mine, it was a well-made thing and away far in the distance he thought he saw the scud o a light. He thought he'd see where it was coming from and he walked on and on and on and this light gets bigger and brighter. Eventually he come tae this bend and when he cam closer he heard the loveliest music he ever heard in his life comin oot o this place.

'Oh,' he says, 'I never thought there could be onybody awa doon here!' He continued on slowly roon the bend and he comes tae this huge room and there all these people in it and they were all dancin tae this lovely music. But instead o havin a human heid, aa these people had a frog's heid. Sae he stood an looked at them for a while and he edged forward a bit and there was one head man standing at the door and he says, 'Come on in, Jack! We've been expectin ye doon here.'

Jack says, 'Oh? I didnae know that!'

'Come in, Jack, and sit ye doon!' and Jack comes in and sits doon on a stool and watches aa the fowk dancin and listens tae the loveliest music he ever heard. Then a wee man comes owre tae him and says, 'I know whit ye're luikin for.'

'Dae ye?' says Jack.

'Oh yes,' he says. 'Yer Dad has sent yer twa brithers oot tae get a bedspread,' he says, 'and ye're tae get one here tae!'

'Aye, that's right,' Jack says.

'Weel, jist you wait here a minute and I'll see whit I can dae for ye!'

Refreshments are brocht tae him and Jack sits doon and enjoys the music. Soon the wee man returns with a wee box wi aa these fancy carvins and the corners were embossed wi gold. Jack looked at the box. 'Och I doot ye can get much o a bedspread in here,' but he thanked the wee man very much and he cam aa the way up tae the top o the steps again. He drew the stone slab back owre the hole again and made his way back tae the castle.

Now he must have been a good while down there, because his ither twa brithers haed been away and haed returned from their travels already.

The auld king said tae the auldest brither, 'Weel, here ye are, son, and how did ye get on?'

'Oh well, I've got a nice one here,' and he stretched it out.

The king says, 'Oh,' he says, 'that is certainly a fine thing. Really beautiful!' Then he says to the ither brither, 'And did you get one tae?'

And the second brither says, 'Aye, I've got yin tae!' and he spreads it out tae and one o them is jist as guid as the ither, like a perfect match.

The king says, 'That's two wonderful things,' he says. 'I jist cannae compare them; they're jist as guid as the ither, but jist wait till yer brither gets back and we'll see if he gets onythin or no.'

So Jack comes in an the king says, 'Weel, ye're back and ye've been a lang time away.'

'Weel,' says Jack, 'I've been lookin for this bedspread.'

'Weel,' says the king, 'let's see it.'

And Jack says, 'It's there,' he says, 'in that box.'

The king picks it up an says, 'Oh there cannae be much o a bedspread in that wee box, but it's a lovely wee box, a very expensive one. That would almost buy these twa quilts the-gither.'

But he opened the wee box and here wis this quilt and when he spread it oot on the flair, it covered the hail flair and oh! it wis like Indian silk wi aa these amazin patterns aa handwoven in gold wi a great golden crest in the centre. The king says, 'Oh Jack,' he says, 'that's the best one! You've got the best one!'

Well, the ither twa brithers says, 'Aw naw, that's no fair. We'll hae tae hae anither chance!'

The king says, 'Look, boys, he won that, fair and square and the castle is his, nae maitter hou pleased or angry ye are!'

'Aw naw, ye must gie us anither chance!'

'Weel,' says the king, pointin at Jack, 'if he's willin tae give yez anither chance, that'll be the way of it.'

Jack agrees tae gie them anither chance and the kings says, 'Right! OK! Yeze'll get anither chance, sae they gae tae the tap o the castle again. The auldest brither says, 'Whit dae we hae tae dae this time?'

The auld king says, 'Right, boys, this time ye must aa fetch me back a ring and the yin that fetches back the maist expensive ring, will get the castle.'

And they aa toss their feathers up and gae off in different directions in search of a ring tae bring back tae the auld king. And as usual Jack's feather gaes owre the back o the wall o the castle. Jack gaes off and finds the feather layin on top o the big stone, and once more he heaves back the stane and goes down the steps and follaes the lang passage tae the great underground hall where the man is standin waitin for him.

'So ye've come back,' says the man.

'Aye, I've come back,' replies Jack.

'And whit are ye after this time?' asks the man. 'It's a ring, isn't it?'

'Aye, it's a ring,' says Jack, 'and the one that brings back the best ring, gets the castle!'

'Weel, it's jist you sit doon there,' says the man, 'and we'll gae and see whit we can get for ye!'

Sae Jack sat doon on the stool and he wis gien his refreshments and he listened tae the braw music and watched the dancin. The man soon came back wi a pure gold box. 'There ye are!' he says an Jack thanks him and comes back up the steps and returns tae the castle. By now, his twa brithers hae come back fae their travels and the auld king says, 'Weel, did yeze aa get a ring?'

The auldest brither says, 'Aye, I got a ring!' and he shows his ring tae the king.

'My gosh,' he says, 'that's a beautiful one, that is a really fine ring. And what about you?' he says, pointin tae the second brither.

'Oh, I've got one also,' and he gives it to the king.

'Oh, that's also a beautiful ring, jist as guid as yer brither's. I cannae compare the one wi the ither, it's jist the twin o yer brither's! Ye'll have tae wait till your brither gets back and we'll see what he's brought back.'

And just as the king says that, Jack comes in. 'Did ye get a ring, Jack?'

'Aye,' he says, 'I got a ring!' He hands the wee gold box tae the auld king and when the king opened this wee box there was this huge ring and it was encrusted wi diamonds, sapphires and pearls and it would hae bought the castle five times over!

'Oh that's it!' says the king. 'That's it! Wil ye jist luik at that! That's the best one by far: the castle goes tae Jack!'

'Aw, naw, naw!' says the auldest brither, 'that's no fair! In the rules ye always get three chances. We must be given anither chance!'

The king says, 'Look, boys, he's beaten ye twice now, fair and square: it's his castle!'

'Naw, naw!' says the auldest brither. 'We must get anither chance!'

'Weel, Jack, whit dae ye hiv tae say?' Jack agrees tae give the twa brithers anither chance in the interests of fairness. 'Okay, then,' says the king, 'if that's the way ye want it, that's fair enough wi me.'

Sae they gae up tae the tap o the castle again and the auldest brither asks, 'Weel, faither, whit hae we got tae find this time?'

'Weel, noo, this is your third chance; ye'll no be getting ony mair. This time ye've tae fetch back a woman and the one that fetches back the maist beautiful woman will get the castle.'

Sae the three brithers aa toss their feathers as before and off they go in the direction their feathers tell them tae go. As before, Jack's feather gaes up owre the wall and doon the back o the castle. Off gaes Jack and he finds his feather sittin on top o the big stone. Again he heaves it tae the side and gaes back doon the steps and along the long passage tae the underground room. 'Och, that's it all up for me noo. I'll never find a beautiful woman doon here among aa these folk wi frogs' heids!'

But he gaed doon onyway and he meets the man again. 'Oh, ye're back!' he says.

'Aye, I'm back!' says Jack, 'But I doot ye can help me this time!'

'Oh, don't you worry. We'll see whit we can dae for ye. Jist you sit yersel doon and wait there.'

Sae Jack sits doon as before and was brought some refreshments and he watched the dancin and listened tae the braw music.

Meantime, back at the castle the twa brithers had returned frae their travels and they baith fetched back a beautiful woman the like of which the auld king haes never seen before. 'My goodness, boys, ye've done me proud. I've never thought ye would find twa such bonny lasses tae grace the castle. I cannae choose atween them; they're baith as beautiful as the ither. But ye'll jist hae tae wait and see whit yer brither Jack manages tae find afore I mak a final decision.'

Weel, back in the big underground hall, Jack is sitting there waitin tae see if he's goin tae get a girlfriend and he's luikin around at all these folk wi frogs' heids and he can't see one woman with an ordinary heid on her. Eventually the man returns and he say, 'Weel, Jack, are ye ready?'

'Oh,' he says, 'I'm ready!'

'I'll tell ye what we're goin tae dae. Jist you go on back up,' he says, 'but instead o you goin up the stairs tae the tap, go round the front and up the main drive and you'll see what you will see. Go on, dae that noo, off ye go!'

Sae Jack does as the man tells him and goes roon by the front drive up tae the castle. Roon there's aa the puir fowk hingin in rags, and, of coorse, Jack bein puir himsel, he's hingin in rags tae. But he continues roond tae the front entrance o the castle and when he got there, he stared up at the entrance and outside the front o the castle he seen a magnificent coach encrusted wi gold, drawn by beautiful white horses, wi shinin gold harnesses on and there's a driver on the top and he had a frog's head on him. And when Jack comes round he climbs doon off the coach. 'Jist you get in there,' he says and he opened the door o the coach. 'On ye go, sir, get in!'

Jack wis feart o gettin in tae this coach because it was dark inside. But he pit his fit on the step and looked inside and he saw this woman sittin on the seat and she haed a great big veil owre her face and her head was covered. Jack thought, 'Och it's one of these frogs. I jist know it's one o these frogs!' But when Jack climbed intae the coach somethin happened tae him, Instead o the dull rags he normally wore. He was wearin the finest silk suit he had seen afore, jist like a nobleman wad wear. He sat down and he felt different. He sat doon beside this woman and he looked at her and this woman was dressed out of this world in red satin silk. Thinks Jack, as he looks at her sittin there wi this big veil owre her heid, 'Oh, ma faither's goin tae get a surprise when I take this woman in and get that big veil off her frog's heid!' So in he came anyway.

'Well Jack, ' says the king, 'did ye get a woman?'

'Aye, I've got a woman!'

'Well, where is she?' says the king. 'Bring her in till we see her!'

Jack gaes and asks the woman tae come in an see his father. In she comes and Jack's twa brithers were sittin agog at the way this woman was dressed and how Jack was dressed as they strode forward tae the king. 'Where did ye get these clothes?' they asked.

'Oh,' says Jack. 'That's my business, not yours!'

The king looks at the woman wi this big hat and fancy veil on her heid and he says, 'Weel, she's certainly a weel-built woman but can ye no take her veil aff her face sae we can see whit she looks like?' Now, when the king says that Jack's heart stopped a beat. But nevertheless Jack takes the hat and the veil off the woman's heid and stood back and oh! what a sight met his eyes. There stood a woman the like of which Jack had never seen afore. Her red hair hung away doon her back in ringlets and her eyes were pure sky blue. The four o them stood staring aghast at this woman and the kings say, 'Oh, what a woman, what a woman! Where on earth did you ever get a woman like that Jack? That girl never came from around here!'

'She does come frae around here,' says Jack, 'but I'm no tellin ye, I'm no tellin ye!'

The king stood up and says, 'Weel, Jack, that's the third time

ye've won the challenge fair and square and look boys, ye
cannae go against that. The castle haes tae go tae Jack and that's
the end o it!'

The twa brithers had to go away and push their fortunes
elsewhere. Jack got the castle and as far as I know he's still living
there yet.

And that's the end o ma story.

The wisdom of the story, and the relevance of it to people who
had to go out every day and earn a subsistence, is that often you
do not need to go to the ends of the earth to find your 'fortune'.
It might be there where you are, unnoticed and undervalued.
This is startlingly apt for today's situation, not just for all Scots
but for all members of the human race. 'The Three Feathers' is
an international wonder tale, in other words a magical adventure
that is found in many countries in versions that suit the culture
of the country. In its usual form the wonder tale is about how an
immature person grows up and realises his potential. It has a
number in the Aarne-Thompson *Tale-Type Index*, a handbook of
the different types of folk tale found all over the world, which
gives every tale-type a number and notes the countries where it
has been recorded and gives an outline of its essentials. 'The
Three Feathers' has attracted the attention of numerous folklore
scholars and academics, notably Bruno Bettelheim. He views the
underground place as a symbol of the subconscious mind, which
gives the story a meaning that suggests we all have within our-
selves a place from which we can draw what we are potentially
capable of doing. Willie understood this from his own intuition,
not from psychological knowledge or analysis. Present in so
many of Willie's stories is the social satire that pokes fun at
pretension, stereotype and materialism. The two older brothers
are model princes that bring you in mind of Burns' 'Ye see yon

birkie caaed a lord' ('A Man's a Man for Aa That'), and we
rapidly conclude that their status does not give them any of anti-
hero Jack's independence of mind. The wise old king, their
father, sees beyond the appearance.

Of course, if people do not enjoy a story, they will not
remember it; any teacher knows that to be universally true.
Nowadays, entertainment is directed at young folk, and has to be
about 'having a laugh'. Anything not funny is 'boring'. My own
experience of going in to schools as a storyteller has shown me
that most grown-ups jump to conclusions about children that
are not necessarily true. I invariably get the younger classes, but,
no matter what their age, they love to have someone *real* sitting
telling them a story, and, although I have been warned their
concentration time is limited, they are anxious to stay on when
the time is up, even though 'the bell has went'.

The same is true of the ballads, which are stories told in song.
Neither in the English class nor in the music class are these
wonderful heirlooms passed on. At an educational conference in
recent years, I found myself doing ballad workshops with sixth-
year pupils from good Scottish secondary schools who had *never
heard of them*. The mistake the school system makes is that they
think creativity always goes along with academic ability: to put it
simply, teachers think that those pupils who are the best at
gaining marks in exams will also be best at writing. They think
any traveller pupils are getting something valuable from the
schools, but they never think that travellers can actually
contribute anything worthwhile, like the maths teacher from
Blairgowrie High School mentioned earlier who never thought
to ask the travellers about songs, stories and tunes. In running the
Fair City Storytelling Festival in Perth a few years ago, I found
on the other hand that all the schools wanted storytellers to visit.
But the evening events that I had hoped families, if not adults

alone, would attend, were not so successful. It was from this I
learned that nowadays everyone thinks of storytelling as being
for children. Grown-ups are too 'sophisticated' to admit enjoying
it. Willie was a master storyteller whom the Perth schools were
privileged to hear, but they did not realise this. Not only among
children was he spellbinding, Willie could make a noisy pub fall
quiet when he began a story and no one ever complained no
matter how long it was. Willie would sit and thread the story on
their hearing like stringing beads in an unhurried manner. No
matter if the dialogue was between a beggar and a king or a poor
country lad and a monster, they spoke in recognisably human
tones, whether they were joyful, sad, fearful or angry. Some of
Willie's stories have a geographical setting, such as 'Up in the far
north of Scotland' ('The Bailer') or 'When I was a young man
and travelling in Ireland' ('The Baby'). But many of them are set
in a landscape of the mind – perhaps based on a folk memory of
earlier times – where roads are long, castles are huge and
intimidating and forests are dense and dark. It is peopled by
arbitrarily evil black lairds, monsters, ogres and giants, bearded
old men and women whose nose and chin could crack nuts,
talking birds and little men in green, drops of water that can
become raging floods and thorns that can turn into
impenetrable hedges. Willie signals this kind of story with, 'Once
upon a time there was a lady and gentleman/king and
queen/auld laird/poor crofter and his wife . . .,' and he does not
specify any particular locality. We enter the world of the
imagination, the Celtic Otherworld, which is vast and endless,
beautiful, complex and magical, where space and time do not
matter, but where magical things happen, huge distances are
covered in a flash, long periods of time pass like lightning. In
ballad singing, to which storytelling is closely related, this has
been described as 'leaping and lingering'.

For Willie, this otherworld was as close and as real as the world of actuality, and immediately accessible. By having this world of the imagination at his command, Willie's stories had other functions than entertainment, although enjoyment was his first aim. Some reinforced family ties, like the stories about brothers – perhaps among the oldest of the tale-types that exist in the Aarne-Thompson canon – and gave insight into human nature that is essential for human maturity. Willie's telling of 'Friday, Saturday' and 'Johnny Pay Me for My Story' showed all kinds of truths about human beings. Some learn from experience and some don't; some are kind and some are unkind; some are wise and some are foolish. The results of these differences are at the heart of storytelling. The stories offer the possibility to open one's mind, change one's habits and look at the world in a different way. It is also noticeable that Willie used the same shaping techniques in telling his family history and his own experiences as he did in recounting the old folktales and wonder tales he had inherited from the past. This suggests that he valued them equally and had the same attitude to them, providing insight into the traveller instinct to have a wise overview of life as all one big picture.

2 Kinship and Family

One of the factors that tie the travellers to ancient Celtic society is the importance they attach to family and kinship. This is shown pre-eminently in the part that funerals play in their lives. Willie's funeral at Gartocharn in 2002 was more like a clan gathering than a family event. A huge crowd of people, many of whom had travelled from other parts of Scotland, surrounded the little country church within sight of Loch Lomond. Only a fraction of them could squeeze into the kirk and I have no idea how it was decided who should go in. Travellers have ways of doing these things that do not show on the surface, and I am sure they all knew who should be there. I had previously attended the funerals of Alec Stewart, in 1981, and Belle in 1997, and remember the huge gathering there was for each. Willie's Bella was buried in Perth in 2004 and I shall never forget each of her children's families lined up and wearing mourning dress. They formed rows on the grass of Jeanfield Cemetery, old and young, quiet and dignified, sad-faced and respectful. The feeling of mutual support and solidarity was tangible. Willie himself was always going to funerals and one is left with the strong impression of a view of family life that is rooted in past traditions and is retained because it helps to keep the sense of family alive, even though it is connected with death.

Of course, travellers also value children and it is clear that in the past it was important for the family to have a growing workforce. They also need new generations to hand on family customs and traditions, attitudes and beliefs, as well as songs, stories and music. Traveller children are very close to their family circle from the beginning and part of the team for the berries, the neeps, the tatties and the hawking, as well as the making and mending of useful articles and the collection of rabbit skins, rags and anything else they can sell. They learn to take responsibility and count money from an early age. Children are loved, worked and indulged in ways that many other children have not been. They are also brought up to respect older people, and to treat family possessions as a kind of common resource. If travellers trust you they regard what belongs to them and what belongs to you not as separate but as something to be shared. Children always kept the best of everything for their parents, but they expected their parents also to give them what they liked. No matter how poor travellers were, they would do anything for their children. I once met a battered traveller woman, old before her time, unable to pay her fare on an Edinburgh bus. I got her out of her difficulty and found that she had signed herself out of hospital, where her husband's beating had put her, to find and feed her children. No doubt she had abandoned them the night before when both she and her husband had been drinking, but even in her dazed and painful condition she had remembered that it was her duty to look after them.

When I was recording the Stewart family, who were Willie's cousins, Alec's wife, Belle, painted a poignant picture of one branch of Willie's family, whom she called the Tragic MacPhees.

I'll tell you of the tragic family Alec's mother's people were. Her mother was Belle Reid and, as all the auld tinkers long ago, she was fond o a dram. It was the wintertime, no very long before the New Year and there was a big storm on the ground and she was intae an alehoose up at Struan an she got a wee dram. Then she came oot an it was a night o blizzard and storm an she jist went a couple, o hundred yards from the alehoose and sat doon at the side o the dyke for shelter and tae light her pipe. She was gotten frozen to death in the mornin, wi her pipe in one hand and her matches in the other.

Then Alec's mother's father was murdered by Irish navvies, that were workin on the Highland railway. He could always get a drink for playing his pipes in the pub and naturally the pub was full o these men on a Saturday night. So one of these Irishmen asked him, 'Could you please play "The Boyne Water"?' But he was sensible enough for that. 'Oh,' he says, 'that's a tune I never learnt.'

'Och get on with you. I'm sure you know it.'

'No, I divent.'

But they kept feedin him wi drink till they got him three parts drunk an he played 'The Boyne Water'. They got his body next mornin: his pipes were lyin broken in bits and he was murdered.

Then Alec's mother had a brother an he dealt and swapped in horses as they did in those days, an he got a horse that was a reist – it wouldnae go forward and pull a cart; it was aye gaun back.

They were up at Fort Augustus by the canal. Instead o goin forward when he whipped it, the horse went back, back, back; an it backed right intae the canal an he was drooned wi his wife and three bairns. It was just tragedy that followed Alec's mother's folk.

Now she had a sister called Bella MacPhee an she was Willie's Bella's granny. Aa the travellers caaed her 'the Deif Lassie'. Noo she an her dochter were at a level crossing in Dunbartonshire. The young lassie was jist a matter o days afore she was haein her

first bairn. An the train was comin roond a turn an the Deif
Lassie hurried across first and never heard the train. The lassie
that was goin tae hae the bairn ran right across after her mother
tae catch her an she only got her in the middle o the rails an they
were made mince.

If ye look back on it – killed wi the train, drooned in the
canal, murdered wi Irishmen and gotten deid at Struan dyke – it
was just tragedy aa through Alec's mother's family.

This sombre catalogue of tragic deaths really highlights the
hardships suffered by Willie's forebears. They were unimaginably
poor, out in all weathers, dependent on the whims of those for
whom they provided entertainment and on luck and chance,
both in trading and travelling, with nothing to help them cope
with the trials of ill health, old age and accidents except their
own courage and fortitude. All they had to help them was their
family, and as a consequence their family ties tended to be very
strong and of first importance to them. Isaac, Willie's stepson,
gives examples of the sort of things Willie did that show the
harshness of his life. He walked over the Black Mount in his bare
feet; he worked on the new road to Glencoe with Irish navvies;
he never lost a fight; he made himself a practice chanter out of a
hollow stem and a straw from the harvest. When his father died
when Willie was only 11 years old, he became his mother's
'bodyguard' in his own words.

Perhaps it is because he himself came from what can only be
described as a large and ancient clan that so many of Willie's best
stories were preoccupied with family relationships and concerns.
I learned from Willie the importance of kinship in his life,
showing the strong connection between the traveller clans and
those of the old way of life in the Highlands and an essentially
Celtic tradition. Stories such as 'Friday, Saturday' educated the

travellers in family values, like those between brothers or parents and children, while others addressed duties in the community, like hospitality and the celebration of births, marriages and deaths. Personal development, like realising what it is one's potential to achieve in dealing with life's problems, is also a strong theme. Willie later came to have a patriarchal status in his family, almost like an old clan chief, and he was looked on with great affection and respect by them all, having an authority none of them would challenge. His family duties and responsibilities came before anything else. He also had the wisdom to know when to speak, how to speak, what to say and when to say nothing.

Some of the oldest tale-types in the world are those that feature two brothers, brought up together but different in character, outlook and nature. Willie told such tales, like 'Friday, Saturday' and 'The Nine-stall Stable'. Both of these stories are very ancient. The age of the story is shown, for example, when in one episode a young pig is cooked by putting it in a fire. This suggests the story goes back to the time before iron cooking pots, which means the Stone Age, a prehistoric time of hunter-gatherers. The tale of the brothers does not primarily concern itself with conflict but with the differences that can exist in two siblings who look alike.

Friday, Saturday

This is a story about a lady and gentleman who lived in a big castle and had had no family, and as time went on, they began to get a bit worried because they had nobody to leave their estate tae. The auld laird was wannerin through the garden this day and he's very depressed, and suddenly, oot frae below a bush comes this wee fairy man.

'Ye're very depressed, sir,' he says.

'I *am* very depressed,' says the laird.

'What's up wi ye?'

'Well, we've no faimily,' says the laird, 'nobody tae leave the estate tae.'

'Oh,' the fairy says. 'I think we could sort that oot. Go doon tae the bottom o your gairden there and look in the well and ye'll get a broon troot about half a pound weight. Take it tae your cook and tell her tae cook it and give it to your lady, and for the peril o your life, don't let any other body eat this trout but the lady.'

So the laird went doon to the well an there was this troot an he took it out an took it tae his cook. 'Now,' he says tae the cook, 'Cook it for the lady o the house and I don't want any little bit o't tae enter anybody's mouth but her mouth.'

The cook took the troot and she gutted it and salted it and fried it all lovely and broon. An it was that nice-looking and tasty-looking, she says, 'I wonder if I break a wee bit off this tail if it'll no be missed.' So she broke just a tiny wee fraction off the tail an she pit it intae her mouth and ate it, an she says, 'Oh, that's lovely!'

She put the troot on a breakfast tray and took it up tae the lady. 'There's your breakfast,' she says.

Time drew by to the odds o nine months' time and this cook gave birth to a baby boy, on a Friday. Then on Saturday morning, the lady o the house gave birth to a baby boy. Everything was in turmoil! The two weans were christened 'Friday' and 'Saturday'. These two boys grew up together and they were just like peas in a pod. Ye wouldnae know one fae the other and the laird just called them two brothers.

Friday got up early one morning an he says, 'Well, I think, faither, I think I'll go away an see what I can see aroond the world an see if I can get onything to do, for I'm sore browned-off sittin here every day.'

'Well,' the old laird says, 'please yersel, son, please yersel. The estate's here for ye whenever ye like tae come back. Ye're free tae go any time ye want.'

So the next mornin, he got up very early an he got his huntin hound and his hawk an away he set sail, God knows where. He travelled for three or four week, an this night, it got very dark an the rain was pourin doon. He's comin trudgin along the road an he sees this wee light. 'Here's a wee hoose,' he says, 'I'll go in here and I'll ask for some place to stay the night.'

He tied up his horse an goes an chaps at the door an this oul woman come out, 'Oh,' she says, 'Ye're there, Friday!'

'Oh,' he says, 'how do you know my name?'

'Oh,' she says, 'I know your name, son, very well. Come away in. Ye're very wet an tired. Just take your horse roon the back an your dog an your hawk. They'll be all right there.'

The old woman fed him well and gien him a good bed. In the mornin, he got up an she says, 'What are ye doin up this way?'

'I'm lookin for work,' he says.

'Well,' she says, 'this is the gatehouse o the big estate up there an they're lookin for a man tae look efter the horses.'

'I can look efter horses,' Friday says, 'I was brought up wi horses aa the days o ma life.'

So up Friday goes tae the big hoose an rings the bell. Out comes a man who says, 'What do you want?'

'Well,' he says, 'I hear ye've got a vacancy for a man that looks efter horses.'

'Oh yes,' he says, 'we have. Just a minute and I'll go and see the lady.'

He's away aboot five minutes an he comes back, this young lady wi him.

'Can ye look efter horses?' she says.

'I've been daein that aa the days of ma life.'

'Oh well,' she says, 'you're the man we want.' She says tae the butler, 'Take him round an show him the stables.'

Away he went down tae the stables an he was there a good long while. He lived up abeen the stables an aa his work was below him. Every day, this young woman wad come down an she wad admire him, for he was good-lookin an he did his work well, everything was first-class. She began to get very fond of him and, to make a long story short, she and Friday got married.

Now, there was a big celebration and after the celebration was finished, they went up tae their beds. Up the stairs, they went tae this room and he, bein a gentleman, he went intae the bathroom till she got intae bed. When he came back, she was in bed, but out frae below the bed came this big broon hare.

'Where did that come fae?' he says.

'Oh,' she says, 'it must have got in through the windae. Forget aboot it!'

'I'm gonnae get this broon hare,' he says. He's doon the stair an oot on his horse efter this broon hare an its goin roon aboot him in circles an he couldnae blaw saut on this hare's tail. He's efter this hare on this clear moonlight night an he's owre fences an owre dykes an owre ditches. The hare wad go a wee bit afore him, then it wad stop an he wad come up an it wad go away again, till it led him away miles an miles fae the big hoose intae the moorland. He lost sight o it on the dark moorland among the heather an the rain startit tae come doon an it got affy dark.

'There noo,' he says, 'I'm daein well noo! I'm miles fae hame an I don't know where I am owre the heids o this daft hare.'

He's wanderin on, on horseback, when he sees this wee licht away ahead o him. 'Oh,' he says, 'there's the castle.' But when he came up tae this licht, it wisnae the castle, it wis a wee thatched hoose. He luckit through the windae an there wasn't a sowl in the hoose, but there was a great big fire burnin an everythin seemed tae be nice inside. 'I think I'll go in for a heat,' he says. So he left his horse and rapped at the door. Nut a sowl! He opened the door and went in and it was a peat fire roarin up the lum. An in the corner was a pig and a bing o wee pigs, lyin in a pen. He sat down in an auld fashioned chair an he's heatin hissel at the fire. I'm awfy hungry,' he says. 'I wunner if I could kill some o thae pigs.'

He went owre an he caught one o these young pigs an he killt it an took aa the puddens oot an stuck his sword in it an roasted it on tap o the fire. The gravy's rinnin oot an it's jist aboot ready tae eat, when a chap come tae the door. 'Come in,' he says.

'Naw,' says a voice, 'I'm no comin in. I'm too feart tae come in.'

'Ye maunna be feart,' he says, 'I'll no touch ye.'

'I'm no feart o you. But I'm feart o that lang-leggit thing ye have there. I'm feart o that hawk and I'm feart o that hound.'

He'd taken his horse an hawk an hound in wi him because o the weather. He went tae the door an this was an oul woman wi her teeth growin six inches oot o her mou, an auld witch. 'God bless me,' he says, 'will ye no come in, auld woman?'

She says, 'I'm feart your horse'll kick me. An I'm feart your hawk'll pick oot ma een. An I'm feart your hound'll bite me.'

'They'll no go near ye,' he says.

'Tie them up,' she says.

'I've naethin tae tie them up wi,' he says.

She pulled three hairs oot her heid an says, 'Tie them up wi that!'

'Tie them up wi that!' he says tae hissel. 'I doot this auld woman's silly.' But he tied wan o the hairs roon his horse's bridle and did the same wi the hawk an the dog. 'Right,' he says, 'they're tied up. Come in noo.'

She cam in an sat on the ither side o the fire, a terrible oul witch. He startit to roast the wee pig again an she said, 'Are ye gaun tae gie me a wee bit o that?'

'Oh aye, granny,' he says, 'I'll gie ye a wee bit o't when it's ready.'

Efter he got it ready, he tore a hind leg off it an gien it tae her an she rummlet it in the ashes an in seconds it was away! She'd eaten it!

'Gie me anither wee bit,' she says. He gien her a foreleg an in seconds it was away tae! 'Gie me anither wee bit,' she says.

'Ye can fairly eat, auld woman,' he says, an he laid the ither foreleg aside an gien her the body an the heid. 'That should dae ye.'

She rummlet them in the ashes and in seconds they were away! 'Auld woman,' he says, 'I dunno how ye saut, but ye spice gey weel wi that dirt ye pit intae ye.'

'Gie me anither wee bit,' she says.

'Now, I've gien you mair than three-quarters o it. I've only got the ither left left for masel.'

'Gie me the rest o't,' she says, 'or it'll be the waur for ye.'

'Ye're no getting ony mair,' he says, an he liftit the rest an scoffed it.

'Ye're gonnae dearly rue the day ye did that,' she says.

She made a dive at him an she's knockin hell oot o him in aa directions. She's kickin him an boxin him an bitin him an tearin him. He roared tae the dog, 'Hound, come an gie me a wee hand here an see if ye can bite the leg aff this auld woman.

'I cannae move,' the hound says, 'I cannae move an inch. This hair ye tied me up wi will no let me go. I'm near chokit wi it.'

'Hawk,' he says, 'could ye come an tear the face off her?'

'I cannae move aither,' says the hawk. 'I'm tied firm an fast.'

'Sae am I,' says the horse.

'Dae ye see noo?' she says, an took this wee lang rod an she turned him intae a grey stane at the door o the wee hoose. So that was the last o poor Friday.

Now, Friday was a good while awa fae his hame an Saturday began tae get worried aboot his brother no comin back. 'Look, Dad,' he says, 'I think I'll go an look for him.'

'All right,' says the old laird, 'away ye go, son, an look.'

Next day, Saturday set off wi his horse an his hound an his hawk and as luck would have it, Saturday went the direct same road as Friday. An he comes tae the same wee hoose in the same situation. Just the same, it was a dark stormy night, an the woman says, 'Oh it's *you*, Saturday.'

'Aye,' says Saturday. 'How did you know my name?'

'Oh,' she says, 'fine I know you and I knew your were comin. Put your horse an your hawk and your hound round the back and come away in.'

So Saturday cam in the hoose an got his supper and a night's sleep.

'Now,' she says, 'are ye lookin for your brother?'

'Oh aye,' says Saturday, 'I am.'

'Well,' she says, 'it's over a year ago he went up tae that big hoose and I never saw him since. He went up tae get a job.'

'I'll go up and see,' says Saturday, an he went up tae the big hoose an the minute he rode up tae the front door, the young woman came rinnin oot. 'Oh,' she says, 'you're back!'

Now Friday an Saturday were like two peas in a pod. Ye wouldnae know one fae the other. Now this young woman thought Saturday was Friday, whom she'd married and she thought it was him back.

'Where were ye aa this time?' she says.

'Oh,' says Saturday, 'it's a long story.' Saturday was keepin dumb! So Saturday come in an he asked no questions. They had their supper an it come tae bedtime. So Saturday played along an went up tae the bedroom wi this young woman, an she took aff her claes an went intae the bed. He took his sword aff his middle an he pit the sword langweys atween them in the bed. 'Noo, this is the thing we dae,' he says, 'where I come fae, the first night we're married.'

He jist went tae get aff his claes, when this broon hare jumped oot fae below the bed. 'Oh,' she says, 'there's that hare again, that ye went after.'

'Oh,' he says, 'that's it again. I'll get it this time.' He jumpit on his horse's back an he went efter this hare, jist as Friday had done. This hare's rinnin here, there an everywhere, but it's no comin close enough for him to get a grip o't. He's efter this hare owre the fields an owre marshes and dykes an it wad run an it wad stop an it wad come back an it wad cairry on. But finally, it cam tae this dark moor an he lost sight o the hare. 'There noo,' he says, 'I've lost the hare. God knows what I'm gonnae dae noo.' An it was dark an rainin as usual. But he saw a light an he says, 'Oh maybe that's the light o the castle.'

But when he comes tae this light, it wasnae the castle, it was the same wee hoose where Friday went. He jumpit aff his horse, looked intae the door an saw this great big fire burnin, just the same as wi Friday. In he goes wi his horse an his hound an his hawk. The wee pigs were in the corner an he took one o these wee pigs an he's roastin it when a rap cam tae the door.

'Let me in! I'm cauld and weary an hungry,' says the voice.

'Come in, whoever ye are,' says Saturday. 'Come in oot o the cauld.'

'Aw, naw, naw,' says the voice, 'I'm too feart tae come in.'

'Ye michtna be feart,' says Saturday. 'I'll no touch ye.'

'I'm no feart o you,' says the voice, 'I'm feart o that lang-leggit thing, an that hairy-nebbit thing, an that shairp-beakit thing ye hae.'

'They winna touch ye,' says Saturday. 'Just you come in.'

'Naw, naw. Ye better tie them up.'

'I hae naethin tae tie them wi.'

'I'll gie ye somethin. Here's three hairs fae ma heid. Tie them up wi that an I'll come in.'

She gien him three hairs oot o her heid but instead o tyin up his animals, he cut the hairs up an pit them in the back o the fire. 'They're tied up noo,' he says. 'Come away in.'

In she comes and she sat in a chair an he's roastin the pig. She says, 'Are ye gaun tae gie me a wee bit?'

'Oh,' he says, 'I'll gie ye a wee bit, granny, aye, certainly.' He tore off a hind leg an gien it her. She's rummelt it among the ashes an in seconds it's away. She did the same wi the front leg, an he's still eatin the other hind leg. 'Are ye gaun tae gie me anither bit?'

'Ah well,' he says, 'there's the body an the heid tae ye.'

In seconds they're away tae, and she says, 'Ye'll need tae gie me anither wee bit.'

'Aw, naw,' says Saturday, 'I've only one leg left an this is the one I'm eatin. I've gien ye the front leg an the hind leg an the body. That's mair nor three quarters o't.'

'Ah but ye'll need tae gie me the lot.'

'No,' says Saturday, 'I'm no gien ye ony mair.'

'Your brother was here,' she says, 'and he wadna gie me the last of the wee pig an noo he's lyin peaceful an quiet.'

'Well, you're no getting this,' he says, an he liftit the leg an ate it. Oh, just like that, she riz! She's at Saturday an she's punchin an haulin an tearin at him an she's gaun tae kill him. 'Hey, he says tae the horse, 'come here an gie me a hand.'

'Oh,' says the horse, 'I'll dae that.'

'Haha!' she says. 'Haud, hair, haud!'

'How can I haud, when I'm at the back o the fire burnin?' the hair says.

The horse came oot an it's kickin the auld woman and knockin her aboot, but she was gaun for the pair o them an he roars tae the dog an the dog joined in. But she was gaun tae conquer the dog, so Saturday shouts tae the hawk, 'Come here an see if ye can scart the een oot o this auld woman.

On came the hawk an he flew at her an tore at her, an she couldnae see what she was daein and Saturday got the better o her an wi the horse kickin her, they finally got her doon.

'Spare my life,' she says, 'Saturday, spare my life.'

'I'm no gaun tae spare your life at aa,' says Saturday. 'I'm gaun tae paste your throat wi this sword.'

'I'll gie ye gold, and I'll gie ye silver,' she says. 'I'll gie ye diamonds that'll mak ye a millionaire, if ye spare ma life.'

'What did ye dae wi ma brother Friday?' he says.

'Oh,' she says, 'I'll tell ye where he is. He oot at the door there, turned intae a grey stane, wi his horse an his hound an his hawk, they're aa turned intae grey stanes.'

'Well, how dae ye turn them back again?'

'Spare ma life an I'll gie ye the Rod o Enchantment.'

'Ye'd better gie me it,' he says and gien the sword a wee jag intae her. So she gien him the rod and he touched this great big lang stane at the door an up sprung his brother Friday.

'Oh,' he says, 'ye're here, Saturday.'

'Aye,' says Saturday, 'she'll no turn ye ony mair. An he touches the auld woman an she turns intae a grey stane. Then he touched the other grey stanes and his horse an his hawk an his hound jumpit up alive. An he was touchin aa the grey stanes roon aboot an ladies an lords were risin up that the auld woman had enchanted wi this rod. Friday says, 'That's very good o ye, doin that. Noo, seein you've got aa the money an the castle, ye might gie me that wee rod.'

'Here it is,' says Saturday, 'if it's ony good tae ye.'

So, they set out back across the moor for the castle. So Friday startit tellin him aboot the marriage wi this lady an the hare. 'Oh,' says Saturday, 'that's right enough. I was up there last night and I was in bed wi your wife.'

'What!' says Friday. 'Ye shouldnae hae done that.'

'She thought I was you,' says Saturday, 'wi us bein alike.'

'Oh,' says Friday, 'that's one o the worst things ye've ever done in your life. I'm going tae sort ye oot for that.'

'Oh no,' says Saturday, 'I didnae mean ony hairm.'

But Friday hit him hard wi the rod and turned him intae a grey stane.

Hame came Friday doon tae the castle and this young lady is waitin on him, an she was gaun mad aboot him goin away for the second time, goin mad efter this silly hare.

'That's a terrible thing,' she says. 'Rinnin away like that.'

'I don't think,' he says, 'I'll run away the nicht.' So efter supper they went up tae their bed an when they were lyin in bed, she says, 'That was a funny thing ye did last night afore ye went away after that hare.'

'What was that?' he says.

'Puttin the sword atween us in the bed,' she says. 'What did ye dae that for?'

'Oh,' he says, 'I see. Is that what I did? Oh ma poor brother! That's what he did – put a sword atween you an him so the wan couldnae come across tae the other.' So he jumpit oot o bed an took the Rod o Enchantment an come back tae where his brother was lyin as a grey stane. He touched the grey stane and of course, Saturday jumped up natural enough.

'I'm sorry, brother,' he says, 'I took ye up very wrong. My

wife was tellin me aboot the sword ye put atween ye.'

'Oh,' he says, 'I'm sorry.'

So the two o them went back doon tae the castle an they had a great ball and a great celebration an the two o them lived happy ever after. I don't know if that's a lie or the truth, but that's the way I heard it!

In 'Friday, Saturday' the brothers are almost like twins, but this does not necessarily cause antagonism between them. Rather than coming into conflict, we find them following different courses of action. In both this story and the one which follows the brothers are lovingly united at the end, the kinder, wiser one releasing the other from the spell that has turned him to stone. In 'Friday, Saturday' the two brothers, the sons of the cook and the lady, show that social rank is of no importance: it is the nature of the person that determines his fate in life. In a sense, the brothers represent the two sides of human nature, and the story shows a consciousness of a duality that is a very profound and sophisticated insight. This can be seen as a version of one of the oldest brother tale-types in the world, which goes back to Biblical times and beyond, with the two brothers representing the two different sides of human nature: the good and the bad, or perhaps, in this case, the sensible and the stupid. Willie was very much aware that human beings were a mixture of opposing qualities and his outlook on life was based on this awareness, an awareness that often enables people to rise above their fellow men in wisdom, common sense and moral stature. It was this kind of insight that gave Willie his position as a father figure among the travellers.

Naturally, the traveller sympathises with the underdog, the anti-hero that everyone else looks down on. It is central to his self-belief and self-esteem that he should feel certain that he can still prove himself. But Willie's mind took in a broader picture than this and saw the weak and the strong, the clever and the stupid, the kind and the unkind, as dependent on each other. He liked the stories that illustrated this, like the next one, 'The Nine-stall Stable'.

The Nine-stall Stable

Once upon a time there was a crofter and his wife. They struggled on in the best way they could. Then they had a wee boy an he grew up a good boy an went tae school. His father let him do whatever he wanted an he would go aa roon the farm steadin killin birds an daein aa the mischief he could. As he grew aulder, he never had any interest tae work or dae onythin aboot the croft. He just cairried on in his own way an his father an his mother just let him, seein he was their only boy.

But when he was aboot seven or eight years old, his mither fell again an she had anither wee boy. Noo, as this ither wee boy wis risin, he was daein everythin his father telt him tae dae, quite a different laddie entirely. The two boys grew up an the younger one did aa the work an never complained, but the aulder one just went an played an he never chaved at aa.

Years rolled by tae they were near manhood, an the aulder one said tae his father, 'I think I'll go away an look for a job some ither place, for I cannae be bothered bidin here ony langer.'

'Oh well,' says his father, 'please yersel. If ye can dae onythin better ava, good luck tae ye.'

His mother parcelt up some food an away he went tae seek his fortune. He walked on an on for miles an miles intae a strange land where he never was afore. As he was comin along a road close tae the side o a loch, he sees a lot o swans an laddies were throwin stanes at them. 'Ah,' says he, 'that's a good pastime. I think I'll hae a shot masel.'

So he startit wi these laddies an staned the swans, but they flew oot on the water an the boys soon got tired. He came on a bit farther an sat doon by the side o the road tae eat, when he noticed aa these wee ants rinnin back an forrit. 'Whit kin o torments o beasts are these?' he says. 'I think I'll tramp on them.' So he brayed them wi his feet an follaed them tae whaur they were gaun, an he scattered the big heap o mould that belonged tae them, jist tae see what was in the bottom o it. Of coorse, there was nothin there but wee crumbs o this an that an deid flies an he just stood for a while lookin at it. 'Ach, there's naethin interestin here,' he says, an gaes on the road farther.

He sat doon at a wee well tae get a drink o water when there comes oot o the well a frog. The wee frog spoke tae him.

'I could dae ye a good turn if ye'd only gie me a wee bit o your meat.'

'I'm nae gien ye onythin,' he says. 'Ye're getting nane.'

'Aa right, then,' says the frog. 'Never mind. What are ye daein here onywey?'

'Oh,' he says, 'I'm lookin for a job wherever I can get it.'

'Oh,' says the frog, 'ye're on the right track. Dae ye see that big hoose away up there?'

'Aye,' he says, 'I see it.'

'Well,' says the frog, 'they're lookin for a man up there. I've seen a few goin up there, but I've never seen them comin doon.'

Away he goes up tae this hoose an chaps at the door an a butler comes oot tae him. 'I'm lookin for a job,' he says. 'I heard ye were lookin for people tae work for ye.'

Away the butler went an oot comes the gentleman o the hoose. 'Can ye work?' he says.

'Oh, I can work a wee bit.'

'Well,' he says, 'I'll gie ye a job, but if ye don't do it, ye'll never go back doon the road again.'

'Oh,' he says, 'if that's the wey o't, I'll try ma best tae dae it.'

'So he takes him tae this stable an there were nine stalls in it. 'You clean oot that stable an we'll see after that what ye can dae.'

'Right-o!' he says. So he gien him a barra an a brush an shovel an a graip an he starts tae clean the stable. Ach, within half an oor, he got fed up an sat doon on top o a pile o strae an fell asleep. The gentleman came back an wakened him up. 'Ye havenae done very much,' he says.

'Naw,' he says, 'I was too tired. If ye give me a chance, I'll dae it the morn.'

'Aw, naw,' says the gentleman. 'Ye've had your chance!' An he turned him intae a grey stane at the door o the stable, for he was a warlock.

Now, back at the wee croft, the younger son was workin aboot an he was wonderin why his brither wisnae comin back an how he didnae even write. 'I tell ye whit I'll dae father,' he says. 'If you can manage tae struggle away, I'll go an see if I can find him.'

'Very good,' the father says. 'Away ye go, son.'

So the next day he rose an got food fae his mother an as luck would have it, he traivelt in the samen direction as his brither, as if something had guided him on the same road. He comes tae the samen lochside, an here were these twa swans an their wee cygnets. He stood an he looked at them for a while, then these laddies came alang an were goin tae throw stanes at them.

'Aw, naw,' he says, 'ye're no daein that. They're beautiful animals, an they're no daein ye ony hairm. Leave them alane or I'll maybe dae somethin aboot it.'

So the boys went away an he took a half o the breid he had in his wee bag an he fed the swans wi it. Efter a while, he went on the road an the swans were swimmin on the loch again. He sat doon by the side o the road tae eat an he saw the wee ants goin back an forrit.

'They're great wee workin beasts,' he says, 'how they work an strive tae keep their ainsel. Wonderful beasts!' An he crummelt wee bits o breid doon tae them an he came owre tae the ants' bing an crummelt mair breid on the tap o it. The heid one o the ants came right oot an lookit up at him. 'That was very nice o ye,' he says, 'feedin us. If we can dae onythin for you, we'll certainly dae it.'

'Ach,' he says, 'that's nothin. I don't like tae see somebody bein bad tae beasts.'

'Ye're no like your brother,' says the ant. 'He was here an he tossed oor place aa oot.'

'Where did ma brother go?' he says.

'I don't know,' says the ant. 'If ye go across tae that well, there's a frog there that'll tell ye somethin mair aboot him.'

So he's owre tae the well an he's eatin his food when the frog came up tae the top o the water. 'Will ye gie me a wee bit o what you're eatin?' he says.

'Oh aye, I'll gie ye a bit,' he says, an crummelt two-three wee bits tae it.

'Your brother was here,' says the frog, 'an he's away up tae the big hoose for a job, an he's no back doon yet.'

'Oh well,' he says, 'I'll away up an see if he's still there. Maybe I'll get a job masel.'

So he's away up tae the big hoose an raps on the door an the butler comes oot an says, 'What do you want?'

'I'm lookin for some work,' he says.

So he goes in an the gentleman comes oot an says, 'I'll gie ye a job, if ye're a good worker.'

'I'm a good enough worker,' he says. 'At least I think I am. I could very near dae anything.'

He takes him owre tae the stable an gies him a barra an a graip an says, 'Ye've tae clean oot aa the dung fae these stalls. I'll gie ye tae this time tomorrow.'

'Oh that'll dae me fine, sir,' says the young man. Away goes the gentleman an this young fellow starts tae clean oot the stables an he's daein no bad, but oh! there was an affy dung an he's getting tired. He sits doon an kind o dovert away tae sleep, but he shook hissel an want away doon tae the well tae get a drink o water. Up comes the wee frog. 'Hoo are ye getting on, son?' he asks.

'I've a place tae clean oot,' he says, 'an I ken masel I'll never clean it oot.'

'Dinnae you worry,' says the wee frog, 'an I'll see if I can get ye a wee help.'

So he goes back tae the stable an he's workin away again, when in comes this wee man. 'Just you sit doon on that puckle strae,' he says, 'an me an ma mates'll gie ye a wee hand.'

He sat doon an fell sound asleep an these wee men got startit on this stable. When he waukent up, everything was shinin an beautiful an there wasnae a taste o dung aboot it. In comes the gentleman an he says, 'ye've made a good job o that!'

'Oh aye,' he says.

'Well,' he says, 'seein you're such a good worker, I'll make ye a promise. If ye can dae this next wee job, ye can have ma daughter, the princess, tae mairry. On one condition.'

'What's that?' he says.

'When she was walkin in the forest, she had a very valuable string o pearls roon her neck, an she lost every one of them. If you can find them, I'll let her oot the dungeons an you can have her.'

'Oh,' thocht the young man tae hissel, 'whaur am I gaun tae get beads lost in a forest amang aa the green gress an breckans?'

'I'll gie ye a day tae find them,' says the gentleman. 'An I may as well tell ye, your brother was here an there he's at the door o the stable, that great big grey stane.'

'Oh well,' he says, 'sir, I think I'll be lyin there wi ma brither for I don't think I'll be able tae do this.'

Away the gentleman goes an the boy goes intae the wood and he's searchin here an there, but he couldn't get a haet! It was gettin gloamin dark an he's away doon tae the well tae get a drink afore going back tae be turned intae a grey stane. The wee frog came up. 'Aha,' he says, 'ye're in trouble this time! But cheer up, man, ye've plenty o guid freens. Away ye go an sit roon the side o the hoose where he'll no see you, an we'll see what we can dae.'

An he's away back up an he's sittin roon the side o the hoose an the sun's just about tae set at the back o the mountains, when he sees aa these wee ants comin an every yin had a pearl! 'Now,' says the king o the ants tae him, 'there's your pearls. You did us a good turn, so it's the least we can dae tae show you a good turn.'

'Oh, that was very good o ye. Thanks very much,' he says.

He put aa the pearls in a wee dish an up he goes tae the front door o the big hoose. 'Is that onythin like the pearls that were lost?' he says.

'Oh,' says the gentleman, 'that's the pearls that were lost.'

He takes him doon tae the dungeons an there's the most beautiful young princess ye ever saw, sittin greetin in her cell. 'It's aaright, ma dear,' he says, 'your father said I could get ye tae mairry if I found your beads.'

'Oh, that's right,' says the laird, 'but ye cannae get her the noo. There's anither job tae dae first. The keys o the dungeon were lost when me an ma gillie were oot fishin on that loch. The keys fell oot his pocket when he leaned owre tae net this big fish. An ye'll need tae get thae keys afore ye can get her.'

'Oh,' he says, 'this is terrible. I cannae swim an I don't know how I'm goin tae get these keys.'

Away he goes down tae the lochside an he's lookin alang the loch, but he couldnae see onythin. He's away tae the well again for a drink an the wee frog comes up. 'Don't you worry,' it says, 'ye'll get the keys. I'll get in touch wi the swans. You come back here in hauf an oor an your keys'll be here by the well.'

So the swans is dippin up an doon, wi the necks away tae the bottom o the water an searchin here an searchin there an the male swan came up wi the keys in its mooth. When the young man came doon, the keys were lyin by the well. 'Oh thanks very much,' he says tae the wee frog.

'Oh, but you're no finished yet,' says the wee frog. 'I'll tell ye what's goin tae happen noo. He goin tae challenge ye tae a race aa roon his estate, an if ye dinnae get back tae the castle afore him, he turn ye intae a stane the same as your brother. Noo, it's up tae you tae pick the richt horse.'

'How am I goin tae dae that?' he says.

'In the very end stall, there's an auld, auld white horse that's awfy thin. You take that horse, an ye've a good chance o winnin.'

'Oh well,' he says, 'I'll take your biddin. Ye've been right up tae noo.'

He goes up an gies the gentleman the keys. 'Can I get your daughter noo?'

'No yet,' he says. 'Tomorrow we're goin tae have a race an you can pick ony horse you want in the stable. We'll have a race through the woods, across the valley an across the burn an back here tae the castle. An if ye get back here first, ye'll get the castle an I'll gie ye a rod tae turn aa the folk that I've enchanted back the way they were. They're aa aboot the castle, lairds an earls an folk wi plenty o money. That's if ye win this race.'

Doon this fellow goes tae the stable tae pick his horse an he sees the auld white horse amang aa the ither horses an he says, 'I doot that frog's wrong. It could never win a race.'

'Is that what you think?' the auld horse said. 'You tak me an you'll win the race.'

Next mornin, the sun was shinin bright an they got ready for the race. 'Noo,' says the laird, 'we start fae up here.' An he mindit the young man o the way tae go. He got on the auld horse an it was just skin an bone. Ye'd think it hadnae a leg tae stand on. Away the two o them sets, an this auld white horse is goin like the wind. They went through the first wood, an they come tae this level an the white horse says, 'Look over your shoulder an see if ye see the laird comin.'

'Aye,' he says, 'he's no far ahint me.'

'Well,' says the auld horse, 'look intae ma lug an ye'll get a wee dreep o water. Fling it ahint ye an see what happens.'

He looked in the horse's lug as saw a wee dreep o water hangin on the hairs o its lug an he cast it wi his finger an thoomb ahint, an there was a loch o water, a ragin sea.

'Oh,' he says, 'he's swimmin through the water! He's gainin on us again.'

'Oh well,' says the auld horse, 'look intae my ither lug an ye'll get a wee bit thorn. Fling it owre your shoulder an see what happens.'

'He looked in the horse's ither lug an saw this wee bit blackthorn an flung it owre his shoulder. An when he lookit back there was a forest o thick blackthorn a flying midge wouldnae hae got through. An this bad laird was in the middle o't! He couldnae get oot, he was tied in a knot. The young fellow got hame tae the castle an he's a free man!

But he came back tae where the laird's stuck in the jungle o blackthorn an unable tae get oot onywey in the world. 'I'll need tae get him oot,' he says, 'or I'll no get ma princess.'

The bad laird's roarin, 'I'm torn an I'm jaggit an I'm twistit tae bits.'

'Ask him,' the auld horse says, 'if ye let him oot, will he let ye go free alang wi the castle.'

'He asked him an the laird said he wad gie him everything if only he got him oot o the thorns. So he went doon again tae the wee frog an askit it how he could get the laird oot.

'Just you tell him,' says the frog, 'tae throw oot his magic rod o enchantment tae ye an ye'll get him oot o the bushes.'

The young man goes back up tae the bushes again an says, 'If ye throw me oot the rod o enchantment, I'll get ye oot o the bushes.'

'Oh no,' he says. 'Ye can't get it. That's where aa my pooer lies.'

'I ken that,' says the young lad. 'But if ye dinnae gie me it, ye'll jist hae tae bide in the jags.'

So he flung him oot this black ebony staff an he gien it a shake back an forrit an the bushes just withert and the laird got oot, an he wasnae worth a haepenny. Then he went doon tae the door o the stable an shakit it abeen the grey stane an his brither jumpit up like life. Roon aa the castle here an there, he was touchin aa these droll-shapit stanes an they were comin oot princes an lairds an aa kin o high folks. An he got his sweetheart oot o the dungeon. He was just aboot tae set off hame wi his brother an his princess, when he says, 'Oh, wait a minute, I'll need tae go doon an see my wee frog.'

So he's doon tae the well. 'Are ye there, wee frog?' he says.

'Aye, I'm here,' says the frog. 'Just gie your rod a shake owre the well.' He shook the rod owre the well an there was a flash and there was a great huge castle where the well had been, and the frog was the laird o the castle. 'Noo,' says this laird, 'aa thae wee ants are my workers.' So he went an touched the ants' bing an hundreds o workers, fairmers an servants o every kind came oot.

They startit back hame an by the loch, the swans came canny intae them. An they said, 'Noo ye must dae somethin for us.' So he waved the rod owre them an this was the king an the queen o that country an their family. An the two brothers went hame tae their father and mother an telt them aa that had happened an the young one said, 'Noo, I'll go back tae ma castle an ma princess, but I'll send ye money every week an I'll come an see you.

An that's the end o ma story.

Again the structure of the story reinforces its meaning. Sets of three in stories often serve to reinforce belief or sense of value. The older brother does not care about throwing stones at the swans, tramping on the ants and destroying the ant hill or refusing to share his food with a hungry creature, because he is selfish. He gets no help with the impossible tasks he faces in cleaning out the stable and ends up turned in to a lifeless lump of stone. The younger one has a kinder heart and fares better. He will not ill treat or see ill treated any living creature because he feels kinship with them and so they help him accomplish his tasks. In the end, the younger one restores his brother to life and presumably makes a wiser man of him. It is no accident that these were brothers in the same family. This story makes clear the importance of kindness in all life and closeness to nature, which is something the travellers have understood far longer than modern environmentalists have. Willie loved the world of nature and believed that if you were kind to animals, they would repay your kindness in some way. He obviously considered himself part of nature and most of his life was lived in the outdoors, either for work or play, which gave him that weather-beaten appearance that some people mistake for ingrained dirt or lack of hygiene. In all the time I knew Willie and Bella, visiting their trailer and entertaining them in my house, I never knew of them being other than spotlessly clean and fresh. They had the travellers' knowledge of how to keep themselves and all their possessions decent and fit for any company.

Living creatures and growing things were very important to them and their lives – as food, as the means of making things to sell and as constant pleasures to the senses – and they seldom missed opportunities that came their way. It is also characteristic of Willie that he could spot a fox slipping under a hedge on the other side of a field as he was driving down the motorway to Edinburgh. Most travellers have dogs: in the case of women, Yorkshire Terriers are very popular, but many have hunting dogs or lurchers for chasing rabbits and hares. Willie's stance at Doubledykes caravan site had a garden, mostly planted and tended by Bella, but also used by Willie to grow willow wands for baskets. He was very insistent that wild willow was used, so none of his wands would ever have seen a garden centre, but were more likely to have been taken from secret places known to the connoisseur and the expert in the wilds of Perthshire.

In other stories there is a family setting, with ties of parent and child, siblings and close relations having a bearing on the story. This is true of 'The Beard', 'Johnny Pay Me' and 'The Three-fittit Pot', for example. It is because of the solidarity of the three brothers in 'The Beard' that they are able to overcome the greedy little bearded man and force him to reveal his secrets. It is because of the need for Johnny to develop as a human being who can earn his own living that he has eventually to leave his mother and make his way in the world. The traveller couple in 'The Three-fittit Pot' acquire a pot that supplies all their needs, a wish-fulfilment tale but one that anyone can relate to and which makes it possible for them to achieve a life they can enjoy.

3 Making a Living

The importance of making a living among travelling people, cannot be over-emphasised. It is part of being a man, to be able to go out each day and earn a wage by doing whatever work is available, as well as make tinware, baskets and heather besoms. The survival of the travellers as a social group has depended on this. Travellers are not keen to save money or have a big bank account. Their way is to spend whatever they earn on their family and friends, then, when it is all gone, they will go out and earn more. They have been prepared to go to wherever there is work and do it, so they have many skills, and do not differentiate clearly between work and play. The *scaldie* job from nine to five does not appeal to them. Nowadays, some of the settled travellers have been willing to compromise about this, but even if they take a permanent job they are quite ready to leave it for something else. Money is important but it is never the only consideration.

Willie had the skills of the older travelling man: he could make tin and make baskets, but nowadays it has been mainly for students of folklore and makers of films. He did the seasonal farm-work that his parents did and probably theirs before them, and he learned about piping by listening to competitions at the Games and also earned a lot of money entertaining the busloads of visitors who arrive every year in the Highlands. A song I wrote is partly composed of his own words from an interview I had with him to get information for the programme notes at Kinross Festival in the 1970s, at which Willie was a guest. In his own words he painted a picture of his earliest years and his life as a traveller, particularly after the loss of his father when he was eleven years old. He also expressed his philosophical attitude to the government's 'moving-on' policy that made the lives of so many travellers so difficult. The song was used in the Winged Horse Theatre's stage production of *The Yellow on the Broom*.

Willie MacPhee's Song

It was in nine-teen ten that I first saw day-licht, In a hoose wi a roof and a fi - re - side bricht. My mi - ther and fai - ther warked hard on the fairm, And they did aa they could for tae keep me frae hairm.

One day when the crops were aa planted and hoed
Ma dad took the notion tae gang on the road
We travelled through Scotland and Ireland as well
And that was my schoolin the truth for tae tell.

On the road a guid livin's no easily made
So I became maister o mony's a trade:
Tinsmithin an pipin an fairmwork tae
And ony ither job that I fund for tae dae.

I'm a dab hand at makkin the baskets an creels
Or playin pipe mairches an strathspeys an reels
I can mend an auld engine or cure a lame horse
And I like best tae camp, amang heather and gorse.

But times aye get harder an when the work's done
The polis arrive and they're movin us on.
O ye cannae camp here and ye cannae camp there
Sune the wan place that's left'll be up in the air.

So I'll tak a rocket an gang tae the mune
I'll find a guid campsite an never come doun.
When you hear ma pipes playin clear, loud and high
Ye'll ken Willie MacPhee's in his hame in the sky.

There is also a video of Willie MacPhee's verbatim account of where he was born, in September 1910 in Dunbartonshire, where his mother and father were doing seasonal farm-work, planting the potato crop. In speaking first about seasonal farmwork, Willie said, 'You could gather potatoes, you could single turnips, spread manure on the fields. Another job was gaitherin clover stones, that's gaitherin stones in the fields here an there an pittin them in a big heap, thinnin turnips, shawin turnips. Of course, ma mither used tae hawk a bit and used tae mak her own baskets and hawk them. An that was the way we kept a livin. There was no such thing as Social Security then, or no benefits for widows then and that's the wey she brung us up. It wis kin o seasonal work. In winter we dune nothin.Ye couldnae dae much in the winter. It wis too hard bidin oot in a tent to do ony work. There werenae much work wi the fermers in the winter time. They must hae had their own people tae look efter their ferms then. It wis jist inside work. The traivellers never dune much o that. There micht an odd yin get a job inside the ferm as a ferm servant but travellers never got much o that. Mostly the hard work, that's what they got, wi very little pey!'

Both his parents were born in Dunbartonshire, each born twenty-five miles from Helensburgh, and his father, Andrew MacPhee, belonged to one of the biggest of the travelling clans. His mother was a Cameron, another big traveller clan. His father had a sister, known in the family as Perthshire Nancy, who was married to John Stewart, the great piper, and became mother of a large family, including Alec, who, with his wife Belle, and two daughters, Sheila and Cathie, became known as the Stewarts of Blair. Willie's first cousin Alec Stewart was his lifelong friend and fellow piper by loch and glen. Sheila Stewart, the daughter of Belle and Alec, said to me that her father and Willie were 'on the same wave-length'.

Willie travelled with his family all over Scotland and Ireland and learned all the travellers' skills, like tinsmithing, basket-making, bagpiping and, in Willie's case, blacksmithing, earning him the nickname of the Blacksmith or the Big Smithy. Metal-workers have always been connected in people's minds with magicians because of their skill in transforming and altering the shape of the material they fashion, turning the ugly into the beautiful. Maybe that's why he liked this story.

The Blacksmith

A blacksmith and his wife lived in this wee cottage. He was a very pleasant old man, but his wife was a crabbit auld devil.

They were always arguin wi one another. One mornin, he goes intae the smithy an pit on a big fire an sat doon on an auld chair tae wait for customers comin. All of a sudden a young man came through the door.

'Are ye no workin, the day, smith?' he says.

'No,' he says, 'no the day.'

'Well,' he says, 'would ye mind very much if I was tae use your tools an your anvil tae dae a wee job?'

'Oh no,' he says, 'that's quite all right.'

So the young man went oot the door an he took in a young woman, aa oot o shape, a twisted, ugly cratur. He went owre tae where the fire was an blew it up till the sparks were goin up through the lum. Then he catches the young woman an pits her on top o the red-hot cinders! When the flesh was burnt off her bones, he took the bones an pit them on the anvil an broke them up wi the hammer till they were just like dust. Then he gathered the dust together an spat on it twice or three times an blowed air on it. All of a sudden, there appeared oot o it the most beautiful young woman anybody ever saw. The smith's lookin at this an he says, 'That's funny!'

'Well,' says the young man, 'don't you tell an don't you try what ye see ony ither body doin, an I'll gie ye five sovereigns.'

Away the young man went an the beautiful lady wi him. The smith's sittin in his chair an thinkin aboot this, when through the door comes his auld wife. 'Ye're sittin on that chair again!' she says. 'Ye're daein nothin but heatin yersel at the fire. Ye'd better get up an dae somethin!'

'Oh,' he says, 'I'm goin tae dae somethin aaright!' an he grabbed her an pit her on top o the fire an blew it up an she's screamin an roarin. He burnt her tae a shinner! 'Noo,' he says, 'I'll hae a pleasin, good-lookin woman in just a minute.' He gaithers the banes and lays them on the anvil an hammers them till they're intae dust. He made a nice wee heap o it an spat on it, then blowed. Nothing happened! He did it again an again, but naw! Naethin!

'Aw,' he says, 'what hae I done? I've burnt ma auld wife. I'll be hanged an transported! The best thing I can dae is clear oot o here!'

He went intae the hoose an pit two-three tools an some claes intae a bundle an set oot. He's aye lookin back tae see if anybody's followin him. Two or three days later, he comes tae the tap o a hill an he looks doon intae a valley wi a wee toon an beautiful music comin up fae it. 'I wonder what's gaun on doon there,' he says. He was haufway doon the brae when he met an auld man comin up.

'What's gaun on in the toon?' he says. 'I'm a stranger here an I dinnae ken.'

'Well,' he says, 'it's a kind o a holiday. It's for the laird's daughter. Three years ago, she took ill an she's all disfigured. Noo, maybe you can tell me something. Can ye tell me where there's a smithy?'

'Well, I'm a smith,' he says. 'What is it you want done?'

'I've a wee skillet for boilin ma tea in,' the auld man says, 'an the handle's come off. Dae ye think ye could sort it?'

'Oh certainly,' he says. So he went tae the auld man's hoose an he pit the handle on his wee pan. 'How's that, old man?'

'That's fine,' says the old man. 'Here's three shillins tae ye.'

'Fair enough,' says the smith.

'If ye go intae the toon,' says the old man, 'ye might hae a chance o getting a job there.'

So the smith went doon intae the toon an he goes in an he spends his three shillins on beer, an when he's half-drunk, he says tae himsel, 'I'll go an see this laird an see what I can dae tae help his dochter.'

When he comes tae the big hoose, there are two guards standin. 'Where are ye gaun, old man?'

'I'm gaun tae see the laird,' he says. 'I've heard that his dochter's been ill.'

'That's right. Are you a doctor?'

'I'm no a doctor. I'm a blacksmith.'

'I doot,' says the guard, 'ye'll not be able tae dae much because specialists fae aa owre could dae nothin wi her.'

'Ach well,' he says, 'I'll try anyway.' So they let him come up tae the hoose an he raps on the front door, an a butler comes oot.

'What dae ye want, old man?'

'I've heard the dochter o the hoose is ill an I've come tae see if I could dae onythin for her.'

'I'll see what the laird says,' says the butler.

In he goes an the laird comes oot. 'If you can cure my daughter,' he says tae the smith, 'I'll gie ye anything in this world.'

'Well,' he says, 'I'd like a wee blacksmith's shop.'

'Oh I've got five or six blacksmith's shops,' he says, an he showed him roon, an there were two or three men workin in them.

'I just want tae work masel,' the smith says, 'I don't need these men.'

'Well,' says the laird, 'jist suit yersel. Dae your work. But how are ye gaun tae cure my daughter?'

'Bring your dochter doon in aboot hauf an oor, an leave her wi me an I'll cure her,' he says.

'Fair enough,' says the laird.

The smith went in an kennled [kindled] up the fire an the sparks flew up the chimney. The laird comes doon wi his dochter an she was the ugliest woman ye ever saw. 'There ye are, old man,' says the laird. 'See what ye can do wi her.'

The auld smith tane the lassie an put her on the fire an burnt her till there was nothin but the banes an he gathered them up an pit them on the anvil an broke them up an spat on them an blawed them, but naw! Naethin happened! He tried it owre an owre again, but not a thing happened. 'Aw, there noo,' he says, 'I'll be shot or killed this time. There's no use tryin tae run away fae this!'

He's sittin lookin at the remains o the bones on top o the anvil, when there's somebody comes tae the door. 'That's him back for his dochter!' he says, but the door opens an in comes the young man he had first seen at the smithy. 'I thocht I telt ye,' he says, 'never in your life tae try onything ye see any other body daein.'

'Well,' says the smith, 'I'm sorry.'

'Sorry's too late!' says the young man an he hit him a welt. Then he gathered aa the bones together on the anvil an spat on them an blew an the most beautiful young woman appeared. 'Now,' he says tae the smith, 'I'm gaun tae gie ye anither five sovereigns, for ye never tae let on aboot this.'

'I'll no speak aboot it,' says the smith.

The young man took the young woman an went oot the door an the smith's sittin rubbin his hands when the door opened again and in came his auld wife! He lookit at her. 'Is that you, Maggie?' he says.

'Aye,' she says, 'it's me. Wha did ye think it was?'

'It canny be you!' he says.

'How can it no be me?' she says.

He went forward tae her. 'Oh, it's you richt enough!' he says an gien her a kiss.

'Ye'd better get your fire gaun,' she says. 'There's a man comin in wi a pair o horses he wants shoed.'

He was shoein the man's horses when he had tae gae intae the hoose for mair nails. 'Have ye nae tea in the hoose, Maggie?' he says.

'How can I get tea,' she says, 'when there's no a penny in the hoose?'

He pit his hand in his pocket an took oot the ten gold sovereigns. 'Ye've money noo,' he says, 'haven't ye?'

'Whaur did that come fae?' she says.

'I dinnae ken,' he says. 'Either I fell asleep or something droll happened tae me, but there's ten sovereigns!'

Willie recalled, 'All my uncles, off both sides, were all tinsmiths. They learnt me, they showed me a wee bit here and there, whit to do, and when I got up I learnt tae dae it tae. I made things and got a set o tools and a stake and all this cairry-on, all the necessities ye need for makkin tin, and I started makkin tin. But at one time it wasnae sae easy buyin the tin, because it was dear. And it kin o died away because, gin ye bought your tin and got doon and made stuff and put it aa the gither and sorted it and your mother or your wife, if ye were mairrit, gane oot and hawked it. It didnae hardly pey your expense. Through time it wis dune awa wi. For there wis no one hardly buyin tin stuff. The enamel come oot, then the aluminium come oot, now it's the plastic, they're makkin stuff oot o plastic. There's no demand for tinware.'

Talking about basket-making, Willie mentioned that his mother was a great basket-maker, so no doubt he first learned from her. 'I used tae mak baskets also. Cut the wands along the roadside, peeled them and made baskets. It's gaun on yet, the basketwork. Ye can aye sell baskets.' To make a basket you need willow wands, which you soak in water and peel, before weaving them into whatever you want, a big apple basket, one for shopping or one for carrying foodstuffs. Willie also told me that to soak any basket in water would ensure that it lasted for years. He knew where the best wands were to be found and, as already mentioned, he even grew them next to his trailer at Double-dykes. I have three baskets Willie made and they are fine pieces of work.

As with most of the Highland clans, nicknames are used among the travelling people to distinguish individuals in a family who might all have the same name. These nicknames are very personal and most travellers do not like them being made public; it is not a good idea to use a traveller's nickname unless you know him or her very well. Some are complimentary or refer to a distinction, as in Willie's case. He was known as the Blacksmith or the Big Smithy, because of his experience working with a blacksmith for two years in Fife when he was young. I know of Widdencuffs, the Rockingham Teapot, Pipe Empty, Brutus, the Iron Man, the Deif Lassie, the Galoot and others. There were also nicknames for families or branches of families, such as Spotties, Brochans, Squirrels, Tearlachs. These acquired an almost totemic power in the minds of the travellers, perhaps because, as with many ancient peoples, ownership of a name meant ownership of an identity.

Willie's early life taught him that everyone needs to acquire a skill to earn a living and become a fully developed individual. In his world, if you didn't work you didn't eat, so in a family everyone worked. In the present day we argue about what we should pay for education, but to Willie education was beyond price, whether it was in a school or in your family, passed down by many generations. This wonderful story, which is really three stories in one, begins by showing how knowledge and skill are obtained by listening and following those who already know. From them you also learn to value them not in material terms but as spiritual gifts, then you learn how to use them, then you actually use them to realise your own potential. It is the efforts of the individual, the maturing qualities that are within him, not his bank account, that ultimately achieve this.

Johnny, Pay Me for My Story

Once upon a time there was a widow woman and her son lived away on a dark island miles fae anybody. This laddie used tae get odd jobs here and there aa owre the country, and when he came hame, he was that tired he just went tae his bed. But one nicht, he was jist goin awa tae his bed when he heard a chap at the door.

'I wonder wha this can be at this time o nicht,' he says tae his mother.

'Ye'd better go an see,' she says. 'Ye never ken wha it micht be.'

So Johnny went tae the door an opened it canny an peered oot an saw it was an auld man standin there.

'I'm lost,' he says, 'laddie, I just saw your licht an came to see if ye've ony place ye could put me up for the nicht.'

'Come in,' says Johnny. 'There's naebody bides here but me an ma mother.'

So he took this old man in and the old woman made him a cup o tea an gied him whatever she had in the hoose an they sat crackin for a while. Johnny says, 'Ye must travel far. What dae ye dae for a livin?'

'Well,' says the old man, 'I'm a storyteller.'

'Oh,' says Johnny, 'that's the very thing I wish for at night, that someone would come an tell me a story.'

'Would ye like a story, son?' asks the old man.

'I'd be very glad o a story, just tae pass the time,' says Johnny.

So the old man started a story and this is the story he told Johnny:

'Once upon a time, there was a king miles an miles fae here an he was good tae aa his tenants, an he had four lovely daughters. Also, this king had a miller and this miller had fower sons. One day, when things were very quiet, these boys went away to look for work for theirsels. They were beautiful, strong young men who could have found work anywhere. They traivelt on for days an days until they came to a crossroads. The oldest one says, "There's nae use goin thegither tae look for work. We'll never get it that way. We'd be better tae split up an we'll meet back here in a year an a day."

'They all agreed tae do this an they each went a different road. The eldest one was a big strong, intelligent fellow an he went along askin for work, until he came to a big house an a gentleman came oot tae him an says, "Well, ma boy, what do you want?"

"'Well, sir, I'm looking for work," he says. "I'm willin tae try anything."

"'Come in, come in an get some supper," says the gentleman, so in he gangs an the man's askin him questions. "Are ye sure ye're willin tae try anything?"

"'Yes I am," he says.

"'Well, I'm what ye caa a star-gazer and I've been lookin for a long time for a mate, tae teach him the things I ken."

"'Oh," says the oldest brother, "that's the very thing for me." So he stayed wi this gentleman an he's studying the star-gazin business.

'The second brother searched and searched for a job but couldnae get one, till he come tae this affa rough-lookin house. He rapped at the door but thocht, "I doot there'll be much work here." A rough-lookin man came oot an says, "What the hell dae ye want here at this time o night?"

"'I'm lookin for work," says the lad. "I'm willin tae dae anything."

"'Wad ye dae anything for money?"

"'Aye, I'd dae anything."

"'Well," says the man, "you're the very man I'm lookin for. I'm a professional burglar and I would like an accomplice, one that I can show the tricks o the trade. So, if ye'd like tae tak a chance an bide wi me, ye could earn yoursel a lot o money."

'So that was the second got a job. The third brother was comin along the road and he came to a castle where people were shootin wi bows an arras. "I'll go doon there an ask for a job," he says. So he sat in a bush till most o the folk had gone away then went up tae the front door. Oot came this gentleman an asked what he wanted. "I'm wantin a job," he says. "I can dae anything ye want."

'"Oh," says the gentleman, "come in. I'll teach you a good job if ye want tae try it. I'll teach ye tae be an archer. Ye'll be the finest archer in the world an win a lot o prizes."

'"Oh," says the laddie, "that's aaright. I'll just stay here."

'Now the youngest brother's comin along the road. He wasnae as big as the rest o them an naebody wad tak him on. But he comes tae this wee auld hoose an he rappit at the door. A wee auld man opened it. "What dae ye want, son, at this time o night?"

'"I'm on the road," he says, "and I'm lookin for a job."

'"Oh there's no much work here," says the auld man, "but come in an ye'll get a drop tea an a share o what's in the hoose."

'So the laddie goes in an sits doon an he says tae the auld man, "Ye'll no be workin ony mair? Ye're too auld."

'"I'm too old for work now, son," he says, "but I used tae be the best tailor in the whole district."

'"Oh, I wish I could dae that," says the laddie.

'"Oh, I'll teach ye tae dae that, son," says the auld man, "if ye want tae be a tailor."

'So he agreed an stoppit wi the auld man an started wi his tailorin an sewin.

'Time went on till it came tae the day when they had tae go home. The four o them met thegither at the crossroads an shakit hands an were overjoyed an asked yin anither aboot their trades. But when they came back tae the mill, their mother an father were dead and gone. So the four brothers went up tae see the king.

"'Hallo," says the king, "Have ye had your breakfast?"

"'No," says the oldest brother, "there's nothin tae eat at the mill."

'So he took them in and gave them a first-class breakfast then he took them out tae the back o the castle. "Now," he says tae the auldest yin, "I've got a task for ye. You're a star-gazer, ye tell me. Ye see that nest in the gourach o that tree?"

"'Aye," he says, "I see it."

"'Well," he says, "tell me how many eggs are in that nest, an I'll gie ye one o ma daughters tae marry."

"'There's four eggs in that nest, sir," says the star-gazer.

'The butler went away an got a ladder, climbed the tree an lookit in the nest. "There's four eggs in it, sir," he says.

"'Now," he says tae the thief, "I want tae see ye goin up an stealin one o the eggs oot o that nest without the bird risin. If ye can dae that, ye'll win the hand o one o ma daughters."

'So the four o them are sittin lookin oot this wee windae and the bird comes and lands on its nest. The thief goes oot an roon the tree an goes up the tree withoot the bird comin off an takes the egg fae below the bird withoot it movin. He held the egg oot between his finger an thumb an the king says to the archer, "Noo, I want ye tae crack the shell o the egg wi your arra withoot burstin the yoke."

"'Oh, but that's an easy thing for me tae dae," says the archer. He took his bow an arra an took aim an just tipped the side o the shell an it cracked in two shares in his brither's hand, but it never broke the yoke.

"'Well," says the king tae the wee yin, "it's your turn now.

See if you can sew the shell o that egg so that it's the way it was withoot the bird kennin."

'"Oh," he says, "I'll dae that." He got the brither doon oot the tree wi the egg an sewed it wi a fine needle an a fine thread. You could hardly see the crack in it. The thief then pit it back in alow the bird in the nest.

'"Well," says the king, "you're clever men, there's nae getting away fae it. Ye've won your brides an you'll each get a farm an when I die, all my estate will be split in four. Come back in the mornin an we'll make the arrangements for your weddins."

'They went back tae the mill as happy an anything an they just laughed an talked an jokit the lee-lang nicht. They went up tae the castle first thing in the mornin an they found the king an queen wringin their hands an the princesses were tearin their hair oot. "What's wrong?" they says. "What's the matter?"

'"When we got up this mornin," says the king, "oor youngest dochter wasnae in her room an there were signs o a struggle there. The windae was torn oot the frame."

'"Wait a minute," says the star-gazer, "I'll tell ye where she is an what's happened tae her." An he studied a while, then he says, "I ken whaur she is."

'"Oh thank God," says the king.

'"She's alive," he says, "but she's in bad hands. Out in the freshwater loch there's a castle an there's a warlock bides there. He came last nicht an stole your dochter an she's locked up in that castle."

'"Oh," says the king, "what are we gonnae dae now?"

'"If we can get a boat," says the star-gazer, "we've a good chance o goin an getting her."

'The king got them a boat an they went away an sailed through a bank o fog until they reached this island wi a big auld castle sittin in the middle o a wud. "Now," says the eldest brother, "this is where she is. There's only one man can dae onythin fur her an it's you," he says tae his brother who was the thief. "If you can get her oot an back tae the boat, we've got it made. But remember, that's a warlock an if he gets you, it's *death* for you."

'Out goes the thief, slippin canny up tae the castle an he made his way silently through aa the rooms, till he finally came tae the room where the princess was. An he had her oot the room an doon the stair an just as he got her back tae the boat, the warlock waukent up an discovert she was away. The boat was makin good speed, wi the wind at its back, but when they lookit back, they saw this black cloud comin through the air an when it got near, it was like a giant black bat swoopin at the boat wi its talons. The archer managed tae keep it off, wi an arra here and an arra there, but then the warlock made a dive at the boat an tore it in half.

'"Oh," says the tailor, "I'll need tae sew this up quick!" So he sewed away an the ithers workit the oars an the archer waited until he came as close as he could an he put an arra right through the warlock's throat, an he fell dead in the loch. They managed tae get tae the shore, shakin an sore, wi the water rinnin off them and the auld king walked oot fae the palace.

'"That was very weel done," says the king, an he took them inside an they got dry clothes an the weddins went ahead an I think they're still livin happy tae this very day.

'Now,' says the old man tae Johnny, 'what dae ye think o that?'

'Oh,' Johnny says, 'that was very good. That was the best story I've heard for years.'

'Well,' says the auld man, 'I'm glad ye likit it, for that's my trade. Every story I tell, I always get paid for it.'

'Oh well,' says Johnny, 'that's a different kettle o fish. I've nae money tae pay anybody.'

'Oh well, Johnny,' says the old man, 'ye'll need tae pay a forfeit.'

'What have I got tae dae?' says Johnny.

'I'm gaun tae turn ye intae a lion,' he says, 'an I'm gaun tae send ye oot through the wuds for a year an a day. When ye come back, we'll see if ye pay me for your story or no.'

So the auld man turned him intae a lion an he's away through the wud leavin his mother in the cottage by hersel. When a year an a day was up, Johnny came back in the gloamin dark an his mother's sittin at the door greetin. He turned back intae hissel again an she says, 'Oh Johnny, Johnny, I'm glad ye're back!' She hurried tae mak him a bite tae eat an he went an lay doon for he was that fatigued. It turned dark, when a chap came tae the door again. 'Who could that be at this time?' says Johnny, but when he opened the door, here was the same old man again. 'Oh,' says Johnny, 'it's you!'

'Aye,' he says, 'it's me.'

'We havenae got much intil the hoose,' says Johnny, 'for ye ken whaur I was for a year an a day.'

'Aye,' says the old man, 'an noo, Johnny, ye can turn yersel intae a lion any time ye want.'

'Oh, thanks very much,' says Johnny.

'Now,' says the old man, 'are ye gaun tae pay me for my story?'

'Where am I gaun tae get money,' says Johnny, 'wanderin in the wud the lee-lang winter, in frost an snow?'

'Oh well,' he says, 'I'll just hae tae turn ye intae something else.'

'Can ye no hae mercy on me?' says Johnny.

'It's for your ain guid, Johnny,' says the old man. 'I'll turn ye intae a salmon an gie ye a change in the sea for a while.'

So Johnny's away doon tae the burnside an he turns intae a salmon an he's away tae the sea for a year an a day. Then instinct brocht him straight back tae the burn an, like a flash, he turned back intae a man again on the bank.

Aa that was wrang wi him was that his feet were kin o damp because it was a shallow bit he had come in. So he wannert owre tae his hoose an his mither was sittin waitin for him tae come back. 'Aw, Johnny, she says, 'ye've come back, son!'

'Aye,' he says, 'Mither, I got back. That was a cauld cairry-on for me aa winter in the sea. I got chased wi otters, chased wi seals, chased wi sea lions – everything possible I've been chased wi! I was near gaffed twice by fishers.'

'Ah well, ye better come in, son,' she says, 'an get some dry claes on an get a wee bite o something tae eat.'

So in Johnny came an he changed his claes an got a wee bit o supper. An he was just sittin crackin tae his mither aboot what was gaun on an how she was survivin for the last year, when a knock came tae the door again. Says Johnny, 'I bet ye a shillin, mother, that that's that man back again an if he asks this time for money for ma story, I dinnae ken whit tae dae. I've nothin, I havenae a fig!'

So when he opened the door, he saw this wee man standin. 'Aye,' he says, 'ye're back again, Johnny. Am I getting in this time?'

'Oh yes,' says Johnny, 'ye can come in. Be just as welcome in the nicht as ye were twa years ago.'

So the old man came in an sat doon an asked Johnny how he got on in the sea, how many times he escaped death wi seals an otters an the rest o't. Johnny telt him aa. 'Aw,' he says, 'you're a clever boy, Johnny. But I'm no goin tae be here very lang, the nicht. I've anither appointment some place else an I've just come back tae see if you're goin to pay me for ma story.'

'Aha,' says Johnny, 'there's no use sayin things like that. Ye ken fine I could get no money in the sea.'

'Oh,' says the old man, 'I'm sorry for ye, but I'm goin tae gie ye anither forfeit till ye come tae your senses. Ye've been a lion, an ye've got on very well in the wud, and ye got on aaricht in the sea. I'll gie ye a chance this time in the sky. I'll turn ye intae a hawk. It'll maybe come in useful tae ye efterwards.'

Like that, Johnny turned intae a hawk an soared up intae the sky awa abeen the wuds an awa abeen aa the places for miles an he could see richt across the sea.

'Aw, this is better,' says Johnny. 'Naebody'll chase me up here.'

So he's flyin here an there an he went further away this time than ever he went afore, because at a pull o his wings, he could sheer away up jist in seconds an come back doon. This year wasnae sae bad at rinnin by this time, an when he was on his way back, he says, 'I'll rest here in this wee sheltry bit an I'll manage hame the morrow's night.' He looks an he sees this wee hoose in the middle o a wee wud, an it was aa surrounded wi ivy bushes an ivy growin up the waas. Johnny flew in an he's sittin on the windae-sill ablow this ivy; it was a beautiful shelter an he could hear everything that was gaun on through the windae. An there's a man an wumman an a lump o a laddie, an awfy jolly laddie, lauchin an haein fun wi his father an mother. An here Johnny sees this auld man comin, the samen auld man that had come tae him. The auld man chappit at the door an the old folk opened the door an took him in. He got his tea an his supper an then the laddie asked him tae tell him a story. So the auld man telt him the same story he'd telt Johnny. Noo, Johnny's sittin wi his lugs cockit at the windae tae hear what the laddie wad say efter the auld man's finished the story.

'Well,' says the auld man, 'that's the end o ma story. When I tell a story, I expect tae get paid for it, so what are ye goin tae gie me for ma story?'

'Well,' says the laddie, 'I've nae money. I cannae pay ye, but maybe God'll pay ye.'

'That's fair enough,' the auld man says, 'that will just suit me fine! Ye can go scot-free. If ye hadnae telt me that God'll pay me, I wad hae made ye pay a forfeit. But ye managed tae be sensible in your words that ye said the right thing. So I bid ye goodnicht.' An away the auld man went.

'Now,' says Johnny, 'if I'd hae kent aboot that, I'd be a free man. I ken what tae dae the morra, when I come back tae the hoose.'

As soon as daylight came, Johnny made direct for his ain hoose an as he was comin tae the hoose, he didnae see ony reek or any movement. Whenever he turned tae his ainsel, he made straight intae the hoose an there was naebody in it, nae sign o his mother an nae fire in the fireplace, just a bare empty hoose. He kennled up a wee fire an he searched the place, but there was naethin left in the hoose but a bed in the corner an two-three bits o blankets. He just had the fire goin lovely, when a chap comes tae the door. It was the auld man again.

'Aw,' says Johnny, 'you're back!'

'Aye,' says the auld man, 'I'm back, Johnny. I've a sad tale tae tell ye. Your auld mother, ye can see she's not here. She died six months ago. That lang cauld winter, she couldnae look after hersel. But I buried her, I gien her a good down-puttin, a very expensive funeral.'

'Oh well,' says Johnny, 'that was guid o ye.'

'Well, Johnny, ye ken what I'm back for!'

'You're back for the payment o your story,' says Johnny.

'That's right,' says the auld man. 'Are ye goin tae pay me for ma story?'

'Well,' says Johnny, 'it's just like this, auld man. I cannae pay ye, but maybe God'll pay ye.'

'Ah,' says the auld man, 'that's well chosen! If ye'd chosen that word years ago, ye'd hae been a free man. But never mind! Those three things you got turned intae, the salmon, the lion and the hawk, ye can turn yersel intae them any time ye want. I think ye'll find that's not a bad prize.'

'Thanks very much, auld man,' says Johnny. 'But there's nothin for me here. I'll need tae go an work some other place for a livin.'

'Well,' says the auld man, 'away along the coast, there's a big hoose an there's a man there an he's lookin for a man tae pick the richt horses an ye micht get a job there.'

'Fair enough,' says Johnny, and away he goes in the direction the auld man telt him. It was twa-three days' traivel an he was aboot half a mile fae the big hoose when he heard a voice cryin, 'Hi! Come here, Johnny! Help!'

He lookit up intae this tall tree an away at the very tap, he saw a man sittin. 'Aw,' Johnny says, 'that man's stuck up there an he'll be wantin me tae go for a ladder.'

'Come closer tae the tree,' the man says. 'Wad ye no like tae come up here? I can see maist o the world fae here.'

'Oh no,' says Johnny. 'That's a thing I was never used tae, climbin. In any case, I'm too tired tae trek up there.'

'It's dead easy,' says the man. 'Come closer tae the tree.'

Johnny took two steps closer tae the tree an before ye could say Jack Robinson, he was up at the tap o the tree alongside this man. 'Well,' says Johnny, 'what was that aa in aid o?'

'I've been waitin on ye, Johnny,' says the man.

'How dae ye ken ma name?'

'Oh fine I ken your name,' says the man. 'Ye better come wi me tae the castle an I'll tell ye what I want ye for.'

Away the two o them went tae the castle an Johnny got his supper. 'I ken a lot aboot ye,' the man says tae Johnny. 'I ken what ye can dae. I've a half-brither, a bad, evil man, an he lives across the loch there. He came at nicht an stole the only dochter I have. I wish ye wad go an look for her an bring her back.'

'Oh,' says Johnny, 'I could never dae that. Why can ye no go yersel?'

'I cannae go masel,' the man says. 'I havenae got the powers you have. I'll get ye a boat an I'll get ye men tae sail it. You go and try an get my daughter back. If ye do, this castle will belong tae you an also the hand o my daughter.'

'Fair enough,' says Johnny, 'I'll try anything wance.'

It was arranged that Johnny got this big sailin ship an men an a captain tae guide the ship. 'Now,' says the man, 'afore ye go there, I'll tell ye this. My daughter cannae get freed till my brother dies. I can tell, there'll be three things he'll say that'll end his life. An it'll be the last thing he says that'll end it.'

Johnny sails away in the boat an they sailed for a long time. The captain was a first-class captain an he navigated the ship in the direction the man telt Johnny tae go. Wan early mornin, one o the mates came doon tae Johnny, lyin in his bunk an says, 'Ye better waken up. The captain wants ye on deck.'

Up Johnny goes an the captain says, 'Dae ye see thon island away owre there? That's where the laird's daughter is. His half-brither is a warlock an can pit a curse on ye.'

'Oh, can he?' says Johnny. 'We'll see aboot that!'

When they cam within five or six miles o the island, Johnny says, 'We'll no go ony closer. Stop here an wait here.' The captain lowered the anchor an Johnny jumped overboard an turned intae a salmon an he's swimmin for the shore. He came ashore an turned himsel back intae a man again. He stood up an lookit aa aroon him an walkit alang this beach an as far as he could see in every direction, he saw this great big wall. Johnny just ran back a bit an he turned himsel intae a lion an oot owre this wall he sailed. When he came intae the estate, he could see naebody, so he turned hissel intae a man again, in case he frichtened onybody tae death bein a lion. But when he came closer tae the hoose, he saw a lot o big dogs, so he turned hissel intae a hawk an flew fae tree tae tree. Then he came tae the castle an flew roon it an started gaun fae windae tae windae till he came tae a windae an peered inside an saw a young lassie sittin in the room an greetin an tearin her hair. He sat at the windae till she happened tae look an she went forward an liftit the windae up a bit an let the wee hawk intae the room. 'Ma puir wee bird,' she says, 'ye must be cauld sittin in aa that rain.'

The minute Johnny got inside the room, he turned hissel back intae a man again. 'Oh my God!' she says. 'What are you? Who are you?'

So he telt her aa he had come through an she says, 'You've met my father?'

'Aye,' he says, 'an he telt me different instructions. He telt me you'd never be free till your uncle would die.'

'That's right,' she says, 'an I don't know how in the world he's goin tae die, for he's that fly that he cannae be tricked.'

'Well,' says Johnny, 'ask him the nicht how his life will end.'

Johnny turns back intae the hawk again an he's sittin at the windae. Ye could see out on the sea, sittin on the big high castle. He saw a sailin ship comin an drawin intae this jetty an a great big man comin direct up tae the castle. 'I bet that's him,' he says. 'I hope she gets the richt answer.'

Up the man comes an it's the warlock richt enough an he comes up tae the room where the lassie is tae see if she's still there. 'I'm still here,' she says. 'It's been a long wearisome day. I havenae had much pleasure. I wish I was hame.'

LEFT. Willie MacPhee as a young man. The best man in five counties.

BELOW. Bella, Willie and Jimmy MacPhee, long ago in Ireland

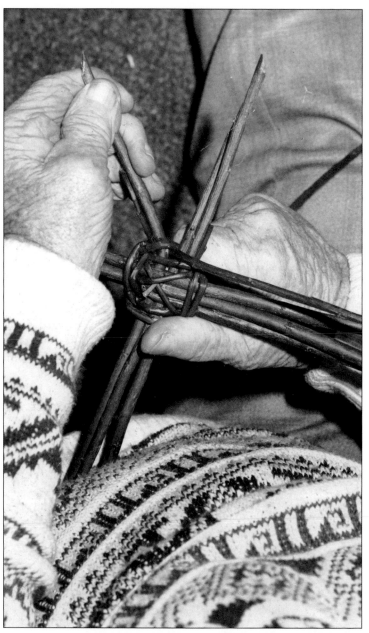
Willie MacPhee making a basket. Willie's hands show his life-long skill.

ABOVE.
Two baskets made
by Willie, which are
the author's most
treasured possessions
(© *Ian MacKenzie*)

LEFT. Willie
made this colander
in the 1980s
(© *Ian MacKenzie*)

ABOVE. Bella and Willie MacPhee – this is how many people will remember this wonderful couple

RIGHT. Willie in his younger days

Willie MacPhee piping – these pipes were heard at many a ceildh

Willie MacPhee pictured at the School of Scottish Studies, where he somtimes plays for students as a tradition bearer (© *Ian MacKenzie*)

TOP. James MacPhee is a relative of Willie's who lived in the next trailer at Doubledykes (© *Ian MacKenzie*)

LEFT. Bella's daughter, Cathie MacPhee, looked on Willie as her father (© *Ian MacKenzie*)

TOP. Bella, Cathie's daughter, who has sons at school in Perth

ABOVE. Andrew MacPhee, a son of Willie's who died as a young man

TOP. Willie MacPhee and Joe Stewart, Scone, 1979: Two pipers talking about tunes

ABOVE. Jim Reid and Willie MacPhee: Two pipers having a tune together

Bella and Willie MacPhee, dressed for 'up the glen'

Scots Language Society's Annual Collogue, Stirling, June 1978.
From left to right; Willie MacPhee, Joan McEwan, Bella MacPhee, Belle Stewart, Andrew Douglas, Sheila Douglas

ABOVE. Louise Hay knew Willie and Bella for many years, and transcribed his pipe tunes as he played them

RIGHT. Isaac MacPhee remembers no other father but Willie, who taught him to play the pipes

LEFT. Cathie MacPhee gave the author this dram cup as a memento of Willie, and the author added the silver band, which is inscribed with his name and dates

BELOW. The late Jimmy MacGregor was a police officer, a singer and an entertainer, and met Willie through the Traditional Music and Song Association

Willie MacPhee with a pipe and his dog, Cruachan
(© *Scotsman Publications Ltd*)

'Oh you'll get hame,' he says, 'when I die.'

'When you die,' she says. 'When will that be?'

'Dae ye see that hump o ground oot there?' he says. There was a green knowe ootside wi trees round it. 'When the wee birds cairry it away tae build their nests in ither places an that comes level, that's the end o ma life.'

The next day, the warlock went away again an Johnny came in. 'Well,' he says, 'what did he tell ye?'

She says, 'He telt me that when that knowe wad be tane away by the wee birds tae build their nests, that wad be the end o his life.'

'You go oot,' says Johnny, 'wi a stick an chase aa the birds away, an see what happens.'

So she's oot wi a stick an she's chasin aa the birds away an when the man comes back, he says, 'What are ye daein, my dear.'

'Oh,' she says, 'I'm chasin aa the birds away for they're takin aa the mound away. I care for your life more than anything in this world.'

'Oh,' he says, 'I'm sorry, my dear, I was tellin ye a lie. That's no ma life at aa. Ye see that big stane there?' There was a great big stane shapit something like a horse, wi fower big legs oot o't an a big long body. 'When that melts away an the fog grows oot o't six inches lang, and haps aa that stane, that'll be the end o ma life.'

Then the man went away, but he didnae go right away, he just went doon an hid. She's doon wi pails o water an a scrubbin brush an she scrubbed an polished the stane. The man sees it an says, 'This lassie must be fond o me richt enough.'

He comes back an he says, 'I saw ye made a good job o that stane. But I'm sorry tae disappoint ye for that's no my life at aa.'

'What is your life?' she says.

'I'll tell ye,' he says. 'There's a log o wood down on the

beach, an it's sixteen feet long an five feet thick. There'll need tae be a man tae split that log, wi one solid blow o an aix. Oot o the log there'll come oot a wild duck an it'll fly right across the sea. An when it's high up in the heavens, it'll drop an egg an that egg'll need tae be broken on my broo where that mark is. An that'll be the end o ma life.'

Johnny's listenin tae aa this an he says, 'That's the third thing, an the man telt me that the third thing's the right one. That's it!'

Johnny flew back tae the boat as quick as quick an he says tae the captain, 'Have ye got an aix on the boat?' An the captain got oot this great big aix. Johnny shairpened it an shairpened it an shairpened it, till it wis jist like a lance. Then Johnny went back wi it tae the castle an next morning, bright an early, the warlock's away an Johnny says tae the lassie, 'Come on, get yersel ready an come wi me.' Once she'd gaithered something together, she came awa wi Johnny. Now they were back tae this big high waa. Johnny flew richt owre the waa an doon tae the shore where the men were wi the rowin boat. 'Ye'll need tae go back tae the big boat an get a rope.' So they're awa tae the boat an they came back wi a rope.

'Stand alongside that waa,' Johnny says, 'an catch this rope when I gie ye it fae the ither side.' Johnny flew back owre the waa an turned hissel intae a man again, so that he could fling the end o the rope owre the waa. 'Noo,' he says tae the lassie, 'I'll tell the men tae pull an you traivel up the waa.'

'Right,' says the lassie. Johnny callit tae the men, 'Pull on your rope!' He says tae the lassie, 'Walk up. Just pull at the same time as ye walk up.' It was nae bother! She jist walkit up the waa till she got tae the farside an Johnny got her doon.

'Noo,' he says, 'I wonder whaur this lump o wud is.' He wannert alang the shore a bit till he comes tae it. Then Johnny liftit the aix an swung it an split the log the way ye wad split a cabbage wi a gully knife an this wee wild duck shot right up intae the air. Johnny turns hissel intae a hawk again an he's up efter the duck an he's crowdin it an circlin it an wi the fricht this wee duck's getting, it dropped this egg in the air. Johnny came low down tae the water an he turns hissel intae a salmon an he's efter this egg. He got it in his mouth an he's just oot the water an had turnit hissel back intae a man again, when they saw this sailin ship comin at a speed past redemption.

'Oh,' says the lassie, 'that's ma uncle comin!'

Says Johnny, 'Get intae the boat, everyone o ye.'

They got intae the boat an pulled hard for the big boat as quick as ever they could. An finally they managed tae get ontae it. But ah me! this boat drew alongside an the man was that angry he was wild, an him roarin. He had a sword seven feet lang an he came off his ain boat an rowed owre tae their boat. But Johnny's waitin as he came across an he liftit the egg an hit the man square on the broo. The minute the egg broke on his broo, he fell on the brunt o his back an lay stiff an dead, an that was the end o him!

So Johnny and the lassie an the crew members an the captain went back tae the ither castle an telt the ither brither whit had happened. He was as good as his word an gave Johnny his daughter an the castle an they're livin there tae this very day yet, an that's no lie.

This wonderful and intricate saga, made of 'The Four Skilful Brothers' tale-type, plus the framework story about the value of stories and 'The Giant Whose Heart was in an Egg', showing the range of skills that exist, and the importance of learning one, is set in the account of Johnny and the question of payment for the story. Johnny discovers that skill cannot be paid for with money. This leads on to how he used the magic powers he won to overcome 'The Giant Whose Heart is in an Egg', as a result of finding the answer to this question of value to push his own fortune. The storyteller, who is also a weaver of magic, makes Johnny spend a year as a lion, then a salmon, then a hawk, to learn the secrets of living on the earth, in the water and in the air, the three elements that are habitats of the creatures of nature. Having done that, he can become a lion, a salmon or a hawk whenever he needs strength, speed and mobility and is sent to rescue a laird's daughter from a warlock. He passes this test with flying colours and thus realises what it is in him to do in life; he is a fully developed adult. It is an excellent road map to achievement in life.

Making a living was important in several of the stories Willie told, even when the work was not the focus of the story. For example, 'The Three-fittit Pot', a tale of wish fulfilment, also shows how a tinker woman sold at the doors of farmers and country folk, the baskets and tinware made by her husband. The roles of men and women were clearly defined: the man fashioned the tinware, did the repairs, made the baskets and besoms, the horn spoons and the wooden flowers, while the women sold them, bought and cooked the food, and looked after the children. Not only that, it gave a bit of an insight into relations between travellers and the settled people. It was clear that the country folk needed the useful articles as much as the tinkers needed the food and tobacco they were given in return. Perhaps not all country people were as generous as they are shown to be in stories travellers told, but it was obviously good policy to suggest that they were. A traveller soliciting for work will always mention a neighbour who was kind in order to suggest that the person addressed should do the same. It is certainly true in the North there was a tradition of never locking the door or refusing shelter to a stranger. The idea is that Our

Lord might return and to close the door to Him would be unthinkable. Everything was not paid for in money in rural communities, where coins and notes were not as useful as oatmeal or potatoes. But in stories, a rich fortune was always gold, silver or jewels.

4 Piping Times

Although his stories and his storytelling were of the best, the great love of Willie's life was bagpipe music. All his uncles, on both his father's and his mother's side, played the bagpipes. 'I always had an interest in pipes. Doesnae maitter where I wis, if I heard the sound o a bagpipe, away for miles, I wad make there just like a wasp tae a crock o jeelie. I'd make tae listen tae him. And pipe bands – I'd follae them for miles when I wis a wee boy. This wis the same when ma uncles wis aa pipers, I'd listen tae them.' Jimmy Macgregor, a retired policeman in Perth, remembers that years ago when the Highland Games were on in Aberfeldy and the piping competitions were held on the tennis court Willie was always to be seen among the spectators, with his fingers working to follow the pipers' fingering as they played. No doubt he learned tunes that way. Louise Hay, a teacher of piping in the schools of Inverness who knew Willie for years, learned the game that the traveller pipers played of fingering tunes on a piece of wood and trying to guess what the tunes were that others were fingering.

Willie's father died when he was just a boy of eleven years, so, as the eldest son, he had to take on family responsibilities at an early age. He seemed well fitted for the task, which helped to give him the authority he kept for the rest of his life. Like many of the men with his name, he grew up with a strong physique and impressive good looks, which made him something of an heroic figure. Although he never served in the forces, his family and other travellers regarded him as a brave man.

When Willie was young times were very hard. One of the consequences of this was that many could not afford to buy a practice chanter. As Willie said, 'It wis wan body oot o a dizzen had a practice chanter. And I never had a practice chanter. What I used tae dae, I used tae go along the roadside maybe and get a big benwid. Ye know these big benwid things, kind o hard and the centre's boss. And I used tae tak that back an I'd judge aboot the length o a practice chanter (I hadnae much experience then) and I wad bore holes in it wi a rid [red hot] wire, tae get aa the notes. I'd mak a reed oot o a straw and I wad practice the scale.' It sounds as if Willie made a series of practice chanters this way. 'I dune that for years an years tae I managed tae get a practice chanter.' This is an early example of the traveller's resourcefulness that Willie showed all through his life. His mother later bought him a practice chanter. Then he managed to get a set of pipes and he 'played the hooses for ma mither for pennies alang the road for tae help us oot'.

When he was about ten or eleven years old he started playing the pipes. He said, 'It wis more or less a hobby tae me. I didnae mean tae play it for a livin; mair a hobby tae pass the time. I'd naethin else tae tak up ma time.' When he started going 'up the glen' as they say in Perthshire, meaning into the Highlands, he would go for an odd weekend now and again, perhaps staying on till Monday if the weather was good. He makes out it was more of an amusement than a serious occupation. 'I'd go up to Glencoe, pass a few hours on the road there, jist playin tae the public as they go by. Ach, I'd jist do this for a wee while, jist twa-three days, then go away and take a rest. I never made a habit o it.'

Why Willie speaks here as if piping up the glens was 'just a pastime' is hard to say, but perhaps the fact that he had such a passion for the bagpipes made him unwilling to include it in the 'travellers' trades' he followed in his struggle for survival. No one should be under any illusion that the life Willie and his family led was an easy one in which he could indulge in 'a hobby', but at the same time his words show he valued his music far above material considerations. Of course, among travellers, work and play are not seen as so clearly distinct from each other as they are among the settled population. The berry time and the tattie time are as much for socialising as for earning money. Ceilidhing was what happened when people made their own entertainment, but nowadays quite a number of people make a good living from singing, playing and storytelling.

After the war, Willie started going regularly up the glen to pipe for the tourists. Bella's eldest son, Isaac, was brought up by Willie from the age of seven and taught to play the pipes. He was the only one of his brothers who 'stuck at it' and became a good piper. He regularly went with Willie to Glencoe and other parts of the Highlands and Islands, often doing the driving as well so that Willie could 'have a dram'. He recalls that Willie had exceptionally large hands and had been told when he was young that he would never make a piper. But his great interest in the instrument and the music motivated him so strongly that he proved this dismal forecast to be quite false. In fact, so much was he a master of the pipes that Isaac says he could play anything he was asked to play by the folk who alighted from the tourist coaches. It was no matter whether it was a real pipe tune from his vast repertoire or some other ditty like 'Yankee Doodle Dandy' or the latest pop song. Many pipers would be either unwilling or unable to do this and would speak dismissively of pipers like Willie as no better than buskers. However, the skill, breadth of influence and lack of preciousness that this demonstrates is in sharp contrast to present-day commercial trends. Isaac also tells us that Willie's pipes always sounded so sweet because he maintained them so well and never took them anywhere unless they were playing well. He could even make cheap Pakistani pipes play well by dint of correcting their bore by burning it out with a hot wire. He was always listening to pipe music tapes in his trailer and in his car. When his car was stolen in Edinburgh and later found burned out in Leith, he lost irreplaceable tapes of pipe music he had bought or made over the years.

Like all old travellers, Willie would do any job in the way required by the person paying him, whether it was gathering clover stones, curing a lame horse or providing some other service. The pleasure Willie and other travellers gave people over the years made them well known in the Highland glens. From the 1960s, wherever else he travelled, Willie always returned to the Perth area where he was constantly fined or moved on for 'illegal camping' till eventually he found a semi-permanent place to winter. This was near Redgorton, where a local farmer let him pull his trailer into a disused quarry near the farm. The relationship between Willie and the farmer was one of respect and the farmer clearly understood the travellers' need for a base, just as they understood his need for security. Both were ultimately serving their own needs but they found a way of doing it that was based on kindness. This is typical of the old relationship between the country folk and the travellers.

Willie's granddaughter Bella has an early memory of standing beside him in Glencoe, while he played, at four years old, in full Highland dress, with a very long feather in her cap that curled over and tickled her nose, and thick woollen socks that were uncomfortable on her legs. Her grandfather kept saying, 'Stand still! Dinnae fidget!' She declares she learned to count by helping to total the day's takings! Willie became very friendly with his cousin Alec Stewart, whose daughter Sheila says, they 'always seemed more like brothers than cousins. They went together up the glens piping for years. It was at Ballachulish they heard a distant piper playing a tune they learned by listening and made it into the story of 'The Ghost Piper of Ballachulish'. This gives insight into how stories came in to being. The story of 'The Wandering Piper' is not only a reflection of Willie's life but has in it plenty of the kind of humour that Willie enjoyed.

The Wandering Piper

This is a story about a wanderin piper. He jist played here an there an drunk whatever he got. He was a kind o ramblesome old soul, an he done wee jobs forbye – any kin o wee job he could get to earn a livin wi, he wad dae it; cairried some tools wi him, did odd jobs.

An wan day he was wanderin away along the road and snow began to come down. It was very, very strong and it happened on a Hogmanay night. So he wandered along this road and the storm was getting worse an worse, an he was getting blowed here and blowed there. An he was holdin his old coat roon him an had his pipes an his gear an everything in this bag on his back an was tryin tae keep hissel warm trodgin along the road. The snow's comin on deeper an it's lyin deeper along the roadside. He had boots so worn they were goin away fae the soles an his toes wis stickin oot o his boots an the snow was goin between the soles o his boots an his fit an he wis fair frostit.

An he's trodgin along an he's trodgin along, till all of a sudden he tumbles owre somethin lying in the road. He sits doon aside it on his knees an he rakes his hand along the top o this thing, whitever it wis. God! Here, it's a man's face! A man wis lyin in the snow an he wis freezin. So he raked the snow right doon aff the man, right doon till he comes tae his feet.

When he lookit at the man's feet, the man had new boots on; split new boots – lovely boots, the best boots that ever this piper ever seen!

He says, 'God,' he says, 'that's a pair o great boots! he says. He says, 'I think I'll take them off, cause he'll never use them again!' he says. 'Puir soul.' So his fingers were fair freezin. He's slackened the laces an everythin an he tried tae pull the boot aff, but no! The boot wouldnae come off, because the boot wis freezin tae the sock and the sock wis freezin tae the man's fit, he'd been lyin that long. So he tried the ither wan but he couldnae get it aff either. 'Oh, I'll have tae get these boots,' he says, 'I'll have tae get these boots.'

So he pulled the man's trousers up a bit, just up abeen the uppers, an the man's leg wis freezin. There were a case o icin roon the man's ankles, the dead man's ankles. He got a chisel an a haimmer oot o his wee bag an he chiselled away the ice fae the ankles, richt roon aboot the ankles. Pit the chisel back in the bag again and got a wee hacksaw oot an he sawed the fit aff, a wee bit abeen the upper o the boot. He got the two o them aff an tied them thegither an pit them roon his neck an he's away on the road noo.

So he forgot aboot the dead man; he never told nobody. So on he went an he was lookin for a place tae sleep. An the snow's still comin doon strong, an he's gettin blowed an blowed there. Anyway, he comes roon this corner efter he wis traivellin for aboot hauf an oor, an he sees a light. 'Oh,' he says, 'thank goodness, there's a light,' he says. 'I'll maybe get in for a shelter somewhere.'

So he comes along an this was a wee farm, a wee croft at the side o the road, some wee steadins an things. He come along an there was this windae an there was a bright light comin through the windae. He keeked through the windae tae see whit he could see. An he sees an old man and wumman sittin an there was a bottle o whisky on the table an there was a great big chicken on the table. It bein Hogmanay night, they were holdin their Hogmanay, ye see. An a great big roarin fire wis on. 'Oh,' he says, 'this is lovely! I'll get in here for the night!'

So he chapped at the door an the old fairmer ruz fae the chair an come tae the door. He opened a wee bit an the wind was blowin an the fairmer said, 'What do you want?'

'Oh,' he says, 'let me in for goodness sake. I'm jist a wanderin piper,' he says, 'an I'm lost and I'm gaun tae be frostit, or got dead, if ye don't let me in! Let me in some place!'

'Away ye go!' says the fairmer. 'We don't want no tramps here. Away ye go! Away ye go!'

An he shut the door on him, ye see. He stannin there, the piper's stannin there, rubbin his hands. He stood for another wee while an he luikit back the road an he luikit forward the road an he seen there wis naethin else for't, he had tae chap the door again. He chappit at the door again, an chappit hard this time. This old fairmer he ruz again an he come tae the door again. He opened the door an says, 'What dae you want?' he says.

'Well,' he says, 'I jist want in. For goodness sake let me in. I'll maybe die.'

'Ye're no gettin in here!' he says. 'There's no tramps gettin in here. Away an play your pipes some place else,' he says, 'an ye'll maybe get some place tae sleep.'

He says, 'I'll have tae get in some place.'

'Well,' says the fairmer, 'go roon the back an ye'll find a byre or somethin roon there,' he says, 'some place tae sleep. There are some sheds away roon there,' he says, 'sleep doon there.'

So the piper went roon the back, ye see, an he come right

roon an there wis this long shed thing an it wis a byre for the cattle. One side o it wis half knockit doon an och! it wisnae very comfortable lookin at aa.

But anyway, he opened the door an came right away in an there was two stalls for haudin the kye. In wan o the stalls, there wis this big auld coo lyin, lyin doon, an it wis chowin away, the way it chows its cuid aa the time. It's lyin chowin an where he comes close tae the coo, it wis a bit warmer – the warm breath, ye see. The auld piper looked at the coo an he said, 'I think I could put the boots here,' he says, 'an the breath, the warm breath o that coo wad melt the frost on these boots an I'll get them on.'

So he took the boots off an he left them at the top o the coo, at the coo's feedin place that wis a kind o crib thing. He pit the boots in there an, of course, the coo wis chowin away an it was breathin on these boots. So the auld piper went tae the next stall an there wis some straw there an he blusted the bale o straw, he took off his auld boots an he got in among this straw an pulled his old coat aroon him. In a very, very short time, he wis sound asleep.

So he slept there for a long time. He didnae ken hoo lang he sleppit. He was wakent early in the oors o the mornin, aboot half past six in the mornin, he wakent up. He luikit over an he seen the coo still chowin away. 'I wonder,' he says, 'if my boots is thawed oot yet.'

So he went roon an he got his boots back roon, the dead man's boots. Of coorse, the feet came oot dead easy, ye see, oot o the sock, the two o them; he left them doon. 'Oh,' he says, 'that's lovely!' An he tried these boots on an they were lovely an warm wi the coo's breath, ye see. So he laced them ontae his feet. 'Oh,' he says, 'that's lovely. That's beautiful,' he says. 'That's better noo. I'll be able to go on the road a bit better noo.' An he sat an he thocht for a wee while. He got his ain two auld boots then, that were all torn, an he pit the dead man's feet intae these boots an laced them up and left the two boots at the coo's head again, ye see. Left them doon there an he lay doon quietly tae see whit wis gonnae happen.

So the auld wumman come roon early in the mornin fur tae milk the coo. An she had a lamp in her hand: it wis kinna dark. She had this lamp wi her an she left the lamp doon. She sat doon on her wee stool an wis jist gaun away tae milk the coo an she seen the two boots an she lookit an seen the stumps o the feet stickin in the boots.

'Oh my God!' she says. 'Oh my God!' she says. 'That was the piper, the wanderin piper,' she says. 'The coo must have ett him!' she says. 'Oh whit am I gonnae do?' She left the stool an she runs roon tae the hoose again. She tellt her oul man, 'Come oot till ye see this!' she says. 'Come oot tae see this!'

He says, 'Whit's wrong. Whit's wrong wi ye, silly oul wumman?'

'Come here till ye see this!' she says. 'The coo's ett the piper,' she says. 'The coo's ett the piper. Come here till ye see this!'

So of course, the fairmer came an he lookit. 'Oh my God Almighty!' he says. 'It did eat him right enough!' he says. 'That's his boots,' he says, 'ett him all but his boots.' 'Oh,' he says, 'we're gaun tae get transported!' he says. 'We're gonnae get pit away frae the world when everybody fins us oot. We'll have tae bury these boots,' he says, 'an this bits o feet. But the ground's that hard,' he says, 'I don't know where we're gonnae bury them.'

The auld wumman says, 'Doon in the gairden, there's a big tree,' she says, 'a big bushy tree there, an the groond'll be softer there,' she says. 'We'll bury them in there.'

'Right,' he says. 'Come on, we'll get the spade, an a pick,' the auld fairmer says, 'an we'll go an bury them there.'

So, away they went for the pick an the spade, ye see, an when the auld piper got them away, he jouked oot an went doon tae this big tree an he stood at the back o the big tree an he's watchin the cairry-on.

So they came back wi the pick an the spade, dug a hole an this old fairmer, he's all shakin. He says, 'If anybody fins oot aboot this, we'll get the jail, or we'll be transported. I don't know what'll happen tae us,' he says. 'We'll need tae dae away wi these boots an bury them properly.'

So he dug this hole an he pit the boots in an covered it back up wi earth. Of coorse the piper's standin watchin. They didnae see the piper. An the mist was comin doon early in the mornin. An they buried them up an scattert the snow on the top of them on the ground, so ye'd never hae kent it and away they went.

'Oh,' the fairmer says, 'come on, we better get some hot tea,' he says. 'This is terrible.' So away they wannert, back up tae the fairm again. The oul piper got them jist goin intae the door o the hoose. He blowed up his pipes jist at the back o this tree.

'Listen!' says the fairmer. 'What's that?' An the sound comes [teller imitates the drone of the pipes, then the tune, 'The Barren Rocks of Aden']. The old fairmer, 'That's the ghost o the piper,' he says, 'that's the ghost o the piper!' An they lookit back doon where the boots wis an they seen the shedda o this man standin. Wi the mist they couldnae hardly recognise him an they heard the tone o the pipes comin through. 'Oh as sure as fate,' he says, 'we're gonnae be hantit. We should have let that old piper in,' he says. 'We gonnae be hantit.'

An they're stannin lookin an the piper come oot canny fae the bushes an he come mairchin up canny an he's still playin, comin up tae them. When the oul fairmer seen the ghost o this man, as what he thought, comin up, he says tae his old wumman, 'Run for your life!' he says. 'Run for your life, quick!'

he says. 'There's the ghost o the piper comin,' he says, 'an it'll have its vengeance on us!' he says. 'Make for your livin life!'

So the oul fairmer an his oul wife run away up the road, ye see. So the oul piper came up an he seen them runnin an he stopped an came up tae the hoose an he stood havin a good look efter them. He opened the door an come intae the hoose, an, of course, the fire wis still burnin, ye see. So he rakit up the fire an he got a good heat and there wis a good drop o whisky left in the bottle. The oul piper liftit the whisky, drunk the whisky an had a bit o this chicken. 'Well,' he says, 'maybe that's set them,' he says, 'a lesson, for no lettin people in at nicht.'

So I think the piper's still stuck at that fairm yet. An that's the last o my story. The auld fairmer never came back.

Willie had recollections of harsh conditions he had travelled through and worked in, showing he had experienced the life of the old piper. His memory went back a long way to a childhood when there were not even the roads there are today. He said, 'I remember years and years ago, when I was younger, we used tae come up here many years ago and the road was quite busy. This used to be the old road at one time. That was the public road doon there. I went across that road a few times, in ma bare feet, wi snaw on the groond. That was many years ago. In 1939 I was here and it wasnae good for this job either here [Willie means that it was difficult to get work there that paid well]. They were making this road here and I was workin on the road doon there. Workin for fourpence ha'penny an hour. I stuck it for a couple o month and then war broke out and everything was closed doon, and I had to go home then. That was it.' The story also reflects some of the many changes that have taken place since Willie was young. Old Hogmanay customs have either disappeared or been commercialised, and chicken, which used to be a great treat that most people could only afford on special occasions, is now eaten all year round. But Willie has a version of an old traveller song that paints a very different picture and illustrates the travellers' belief that affluence should be shared.

Big Jimmy Drummond

O my name it is big Jimmy Drummond
My name I will never deny
I will moolie the gannies in dizzens
For there'll be naebody there for tae tell.

chorus: And if ever I dae bing a-chorin
I'll be shair tae gang for masel.
I will moolie the gannies in dizzens
For there'll be naebody there for tae tell.

Last nicht I lay in the cauld granzie
The nicht I'll lie in the cauld jail.
My mort and my kinchins are scattered
And I dinna jan whaur they may be.

Another example of modern affluence even affected travellers piping up the glens. Jimmy Macgregor remembers meeting Willie and Bella and two other travellers at Rannoch Station, on the way up to Fort William, and saying to Willie, 'I thocht ye'd be piping in the glen at this time o year.' Willie's reply was, 'Weel, I would ha been, if the weather was better. But I've got the good gear now, and it cost a lot o money, so I hae tae look efter it. I dinnae play when it's heavy rain!' And, of course, the tourist buses don't stop and let the passengers disembark when it's raining, so the piper would probably be getting soaked for nothing. When the tourist buses did draw up and decant their passengers, they all wanted to talk to the piper, who seemed to personify their romantic picture of Scotland.

Young Bella laughs as she describes the ribaldry that surrounded the mystery of what was worn under the kilt and how Willie at times would play up to this. Once, when ladies were trying to peep discreetly, he made them blush by raising one leg and putting his foot on a rock. Bella also once caught a glimpse out of the corner of her eye of something moving near Willie's feet and was able to surprise someone with a camera crawling up a heathery bank to snap some evidence. Willie remembers one man who came and asked him if he would play 'Amazing Grace'. Willie agreed and then the man asked if he would mind if his wife sang with him. She was an opera singer and her voice was louder than the pipes. Isaac remembers a similar incident when a coach drew up and disgorged a whole choir from Australia that was on a concert tour of Scotland. Again it was, of course, 'Amazing Grace' that was requested.

Willie first married his cousin Mary in the 1930s and they had five children. His eldest son, Willie, died young. His other children included two daughters, Helen (Nellie) and Isabella (Bella). When Mary died it was natural that he thought of finding a new partner, as traveller men are not accustomed to managing domestic matters. I learned that from Belle Stewart, who explained to me the irony of taking traveller children into local authority care when their father died. It was in fact the traveller women who cared for the family, including selling their husbands' wares, buying the food, cooking it, washing the clothes and managing the housekeeping. In addition to this, she might be able to make useful articles like baskets (Willie's mother was a great maker of baskets) and she certainly would make artificial or 'widden' flowers. Belle Stewart's mother gathered rags, sold haberdashery and begged. These are just another way of making a living and carry no shame. In tent or trailer, just as in a house, a lot of skill is needed to do all this. I remember the admiration I felt for Bella when I saw her doing her washing out of doors at Redgorton on a cold February morning, with a washtub, and washboard and an Acme wringer fastened onto a gate, when the temperature made my fingers ache just standing watching her. Incredibly she told me that she *enjoyed* this.

After a restless period, Willie had eventually settled down with Bella, another cousin, whose husband, also a Willie MacPhee, had been a sergeant in the army. He had died after the Second World War, from a serious head injury received in an accident while doing seasonal farm-work. Bella already had a family to her husband, including Isaac and Cathie, whom Willie brought up as his own. 'Willie brought me up from the age of seven,' Isaac told me, 'I never knew any other father but him.' He had known Willie before his own father was killed. As Isaac was born in 1956, this dates Willie's new partnership from 1963. Cathie also makes the point that she had known Willie all her life and as far as she is concerned, he was the only father she could really remember.

Louise Hay was drawn into the piping community by Willie. From Blairgowrie, and now a teacher of piping, Louise remembers first encountering Willie when she was tuning up to play in the Junior Piping competition at Strathmiglo Games when she was fourteen years old in 1994. She thought Willie spoke to her because he wanted to know what kind of pipe bag she had, but I think it was more likely that he liked the sound of this young piper and, as with many others, he wanted to give her encouragement. She had just been provided with a modern synthetic pipe bag by her parents, which promoted Willie to tell her that, 'You get a better sound from the sheepskin. I always use the sheepskin myself.' Young as she was, she must have realised that she was speaking to someone who was worth knowing. As always Bella was at his side and Louise remembers thinking to herself what a distinctive couple they looked.

Later, after she had competed, her mother said, 'There's that couple again,' and she saw them on the Games field, sitting listening to the piping competitions. 'His fingers were going so I knew he was a piper. In speaking about seasoning the pipe bag, he mentioned honey. I had never heard of using honey to season a pipe bag; it was just the seasoning you buy in a tin for me. He had a look at the new bag and said again, "Naw, sheepskin's the best. I get a better sound off a sheepskin." He was asking lots of questions about my pipes, like what kind of valve I had in the blow-piece to stop the air coming back out. I had a latex valve, which was also a modern development to go with the bag I had. He said, "I used to cut the leather out of an old pair of shoes, shape it into a circle with a tie and use the tie to hemp it onto the the pipes." One of Willie's family told me they used the white of an egg to keep the sheepskin airtight, but he also mentioned honey to me. He also made a comment, which I did not understand at the time. "You've got the music in you," he said, "you just have to bring it out." I was only fourteen at the time, and I thought it was a strange thing to say, but it makes sense now!'

She found that after that she saw him at all the Games and made a point of seeking him out and being in his company. When she was eighteen she became a piping student of the Scottish Music Course at the Royal Scottish Acadamy of Music and Drama in Glasgow. While she was there she attended a piping recital at the Piping Centre in McPhater Street, and she saw that Willie was there with members of his family. By that time she had read my book *The Sang's the Thing* in which Willie's life story appeared along with songs he liked to sing. She ran to her locker and brought her copy for Willie to sign, now quite aware that she was in the presence of a great man.

She told me that one of the gatherings she most liked being part of was the one held annually in the George Inn at Inverary the night before the Games. Willie and his family, which included Alec (Ecky) and Isa (Isy) MacPhee, a great couple whom I have met at the homes of Belle and Alec Stewart and Alec's brother John, were there. Louise now plays pipes she obtained from Ecky. I have a tape of songs I recorded from Isy at John Stewart's house in Perth. She was a passionate singer, who put the *coinneadh* (a traveller word from Gaelic meaning, according to Dr John MacInnes, 'an edge or intensity of melody') into old songs, as did the late Duncan MacPhee, who had a rich strong voice. Louise remembers Isy speaking of the travellers as bearers of tradition, showing an awareness of the past and of the importance of continuing to sing and play the music. The gathering at the George Inn was mainly for pipers and usually the MacPhees sat in what was known, for some reason, as Bullshit Corner and passed one set of pipes round for the various players to have a shot. Louise was the little quiet girl who sat and listened to everything.

One night she talked to an old lady from Lochgilphead, who was Willie's aunt and who gave her a ring. The old lady explained to her that the custom of asking for a tune to be played at the same time as giving money to the piper was an old custom. Louise had been embarrassed to take money from people who didn't have all that much, but this taught her to accept it gracefully, if she did not wish to cause offence.

On at least one night she was invited back to one of the trailers, after the session was finished. There were more tunes and more songs and on one occasion Willie told a story, which Louise describes as a wonderful experience. She was so amazed by Willie's riveting style and the completely focussed circle of listeners that she remembers the story only as something that gripped her attention like a magic spell. She also remembers that many of the travellers made a point of reading their Bibles, in the privacy of their trailers.

Willie has left other legacies other than the effect he's had on people and the memories he's left them with. It was not unusual for pipers to compose tunes, and to dedicate them to people they loved or admired. Many of the Stewart pipers, including old John, Alec's and John's father, had left tunes behind them. Alec himself and Willie composed a tune between them dedicated to their wives and called 'The Belles of Loch Lochy'. Alec wrote the first part of the tune and Willie the second, which actually had two parts. This transcription of it was made by the late Martyn Bennett, whom Willie knew from boyhood. It was Willie who first told him, 'These are piper's fingers, son.' The transcription first appeared in *Tocher* magazine, a publication drawing from archive material held at the School of Scottish Studies.

The Belles of Loch Lochy

Amazing Grace

Bog an Lochan

The Devil Among the Tailors

The Devil in the Kitchen

The High Road to Linton

The Man from Skye

The Old Woman's Dance

The Stirlingshire Militia

Susan MacLeod

5 Tales of the Unexpected

Always in the traveller's life there is an underlying belief that anything can happen, and usually does. Luck, chance and fate all seem to play a part, and Willie MacPhee's philosophy was stoical about the disasters that befell him. Apart from losing both his sons at an early age, he also had a disastrous year in 1993 when he lost his caravan in the floods in Perth. There is a long history of flooding in Perth, the town's position between the head of a tidal firth and the melting snows from Highland Perthshire providing a meeting point for the tide and the thaw. The water spreads over fields, turning the North Inch into a loch. In George Penny's *Traditions of Perth*, which has its limitations as a 'proper' history, but which is a mine of first-hand experience, there are numerous anecdotes about people caught in previous floods. The one I like is about the grandfather, who was about to teach his grandchildren the *sean truibheas* (literally 'bad trousers'), a dance that became fashionable as a response to the 1746 Act of Proscription which forbade the wearing of Highland dress. They were on the ground floor of one of the houses, overlooking the North Inch, when the flood broke through his door and they were forced to seek refuge by taking to the stairs until eventually they reached the roof. I can remember driving into Perth across the Telford Bridge and seeing the North Inch completely under water.

In January 1993, six or seven caravans, including Willie's, had been pulled off the site at Doubledykes caravan site at Inveralmond and on to a neighbouring field to allow the council's workmen to refurbish the washing/toilet blocks on the hard stances. Then disaster struck:

The Flood at Doubledykes

In the cru - el __ month o Ja - nu - a - ry in the year o nine-ty three, __ 'Twas then a great mis - fo - r - tune be - fell __ big Wil - lie Mac - Phee, __ When the rag - ing Ri - ver A - l - mond burst thro __ his trai - ler __ door __ And scat - tered his pos - ses - sions to be lost for __ e - ver more __

The water was mixed with mud and sewage and what was finally rescued was not worth much, except for his beloved (and valuable) bagpipes that a 'wee boy' plunged in and managed to save. In the ensuing weeks the travellers had to fight for compensation from the council while householders in the Muirton scheme, just beside the Inveralmond Industrial Estate that lay next to the caravan site, got compensation without argument. They also got the use of caravans owned by the provost's husband's company; the traveller's weren't put up. Willie and Bella had a small caravan brought by relatives from Falkirk that they had to use till they found a replacement. The council compensated them but only to the cost of the caravan they had lost. The housing scheme is built on what had been farming land where, as older inhabitants of Perth remember, the farmers would not put their cattle outside in winter in case of flooding. It was near this scheme where the council had constructed the caravan site.

I accompanied Willie to the Housing Department in Perth and was struck by the respect and the sympathy with which Willie was treated. I kept quiet because I knew Willie could put his own case firmly but courteously. Amongst other things they told him that a lawyer had been called in to claim compensation for the travellers. The council eventually relented and allowed the travellers to get caravans that had to be of the same value as those that were lost. Of course Willie, being such an honest man, declared the true value of his trailer. He also, in his eighties, had to find a replacement himself by driving up and down to places where he thought he could get one.

Later that year his car was stolen in Edinburgh while he and Bella were taking part in a storytelling event in the Netherbow Theatre with my late husband Andrew and myself. After the evening event, we had gone to The Tass pub near the Netherbow, to continue our talk with people who had listened to our stories. After a while, we said goodnight and went round to where Willie had parked the car. But it was gone! He had only had the car a few days and could not remember the registration number to report it missing to the police. He had to phone his grandson to get the number and the four of us had to wait about on the steps of the Netherbow Arts Centre until young Willie came down from Perth to take us home. My husband assumed Willie would have insured his car, but he hadn't got round to switching the insurance from his old car. I was ready to burst into tears but Willie said, 'It's no use crying over spilt milk, Sheila.' The car was found a week later in Leith, burned out. That worried Willie less than the fact that irreplaceable tapes had been destroyed in the fire. His life, particularly his early life, calls to mind Belle Stewart's tale of the Tragic MacPhees, but he maintained his firm belief in never complaining or dwelling on misfortune.

I think this attitude is common to most travellers and makes them ready to make the best of things. John Stewart once told me of 'the best deal ever I lost'. He found a number of targets used by the army for firing practice abandoned on a beach at Montrose. He was making haste to secure what would have been a valuable load of scrap when he discovered he had not a suitable vehicle for the purpose that would not sink into, or get stuck in, the sand. He had to leave the targets and made nothing out of them, but he shrugged it off as one of those experiences you can't do anything about. There would be other opportunities.

In John and Alec's brother Andrew's story 'Geordie MacPhee', a travelling man, by magical means, becomes a laird with a big house and an estate, and a wonderful satire is created that shows a lot of insight into the human condition. The lawyer, who has been ready to kick the ragged tinker man out, changes his tune when he sees the money, and then kowtows to the new laird, tugging his forelock and calling him 'M'lord'. He feathers his own nest by putting himself in charge of the new laird's affairs and encouraging him to spend money. The new laird gets new clothes for himself and his family, doubles his servants' wages and invites all his friends and relations to camp on the lawns and gardens of the estate. He treats them all in the pub and they get so drunk that in their dealing they are trying 'to sell horses with three legs' and succeeding because their fellow traders are as drunk as they are. When the old laird and his lady revisit their old home, he offers them a bottle of beer and some braxy ham. Now he is only doing what any travellers would do with a lot of money, sharing his good fortune with others, but of course the 'country hantle' would see this as proof of his fecklessness. In the end, the money runs out and he goes back on the road without complaint.

The characters in Willie's stories have the same traits as the more intelligent travellers, which are basically no different from those of the rest of humanity. They make the best of things, whatever happens, take whatever chances they get and get up again and again when fate knocks them down. It's easy to call them chancers but I prefer to see them as survivors. The three brothers in the story called 'The Beard', which is printed in full later, show the importance of family solidarity in the face of tribulation. The tale also shows the importance of being able to fight to overcome a difficult opponent. In fact, Isaac mentions his father's 'good right hook', pointing to one of the secrets of Willie's own authority, although Andrew and I never saw this in practice during the time we knew him. By the time I knew him a look was enough.

When Willie told this next story in my house at Scone in 1974, he kept a straight face throughout, although people were rolling on the floor with laughter. He had no idea that his story was a version of an international tale-type that is known in both Scotland and Ireland and has many versions, a tale-type called 'The Man who had No Story to Tell'. Although Willie tells it in the first person, in this case that was part of the storytelling technique he often used to give stories more impact; it is hard to imagine Willie at any point in his life not having a story to tell.

The Bailer

When I was a young man, I used to go here, there and everywhere doing almost everything and I used to work on a lot o fairms. I happened to land away up in the north o Scotland on this fairm sittin away up on the hillside and I asked the man for a job. 'Well,' he says, 'ye're a big, strong-lookin laddie an I think ye could dae a good day's work, so I'll try ye out.'

'Very good,' I says. 'I'll be willin tae dae the best I can.'

It was the beginning of the year when I come there, and I did a whole summer's work right through tae the hairvest time. I managed tae build stacks and everything like that, and we got in wur hairvest. When the hairvest was finished, they held a ceilidh an everyone was tellin stories or singin sangs or playin pipes an fiddles, but I couldnae dae onythin like that. But I sat in the corner enjoyin it aa. After everyone had done something, a song or a story or a tune, the fairmer says tae me, 'Look Willie, dae ye not think its time ye were daein a wee bit turn?'

'I cannae tell stories,' I says, 'an I cannae sing sangs. I cannae play pipes. I can dae naethin like that. I'm useless.'

'Well, in that case,' he says, 'dae ye mind daein a wee forfeit?'

'Oh no,' I says, 'I dinnae mind.'

'Well,' he says, 'ye ken where the old boat is doon on the shore?'

'Aye,' I says.

'Ye know the bailer for bailin oot the water oot o the boat?'

'Yes, I know it well.'

'Well, I want that bailer tae use tae measure oot the feed for the cattle, the morn,' says the fairmer. 'Just you go doon there an get it an bring it back up here.'

'Aw,' I says, 'that's an easy forfeit.'

I buttoned up ma jaicket an goes through the door. It was dark, so the fairmer gien me a lantern tae show me the way doon. It would be aboot a hundred yairds fae the fairm where the boat was lyin on the shore. 'Oh there it is,' I says. 'This is dead easy.'

I left the lamp doon an went intae the boat and walkit wi ma big heavy boots tae the end o the boat. I bent doon tae get the bailer an ma feet slippit and I fell on ma heid an I saw stars! When I came to, I gropit aboot an got the bailer an pit ma leg owre the bow o the boat tae get oot on the shore, and I couldnae find the bottom!

'What's happened here?' I says. I got one o the oars and I gropit wi it tae see if I could feel the deepness, but naw! 'I ken what's happened,' I says, 'my weight in the end o the boat has made it slip oot on the water.' I lookit roon but it was quite dark. I couldnae even see ma light and the waves were beginning tae shoot up. 'I'll get the oars oot,' I says, 'an row back tae the shore.'

I was a good strong man at the time, so I got the oars and I'm oarin away and oarin away, but nae sign o the beach at aa. I couldnae get intae the shore an the waves were getting bigger and my arms felt weak, I could hardly pull the oars.

'Goodness, that's terrible,' I says, 'I'll need tae tak a smoke o ma pipe.' So I pulled the oars in an put ma hand up tae get ma pipe, and I felt the big lump. 'Hullo,' I says, 'What's wrong here?' I felt the other side. I had two big lumps! 'Wait a minute,' I says, 'there's something cock-eyed here!' Instead o ma big auld jaicket, it was a woman's blouse that was on me. I put my hand up tae scart ma heid, and I felt beautiful long hair, right back like this. On ma legs, instead o troosers, it was a skirt that was on me. An somethin had gone – it was away! Replaced wi something else!

I sat aa numbed: I didnae ken what tae think. But the waves is getting worse an when I tried tae row, I couldnae use two oars, I could only use one at a time. I got so exhausted, I fell intae the back o the boat an I lay there sobbin an greetin. I don't know how long I lay there, but when I awakened the sun was shinin an the boat was at a standstill. I lookit aroon an it wisnae my shore, it was a different shore entirely. 'What's goin tae happen tae me?' I says.

'Hallo, where did you come from, my dear?'

'I don't know,' I says, 'I was shipwrecked I think.' I had tae make up a story.

'Ye better come home wi me an get some dry clothin,' he says.

So I came tae the hoose, a beautiful hoose. 'There's not many women here,' he says. 'There's nae lady o the hoose, jist servants and some ither crofters. I'm the only body that's here. Dry your clothes an I'll see about dinner.'

'Fair enough,' I says.

So I got a big towel roon me an I got my clothes dry at the fire. Then he asks again, 'Where do ye come from?'

'I don't know where I come from. I don't know what happened to me.'

'Well,' he says, 'the best thing ye can do is stay here for a while. Somebody of your people'll look for ye. Just stay here.'

So I stayed for a long time and this young man fell in love wi me. It's only natural, isn't it? We got married and, as time rolled by, what should happen tae a married couple happened tae us. We had two o a family.

When they were about seven and nine years old, we were oot walkin one day and we wandered doon richt tae the point where I had come in on the boat.

'There's the old boat,' he says, 'that ye came here in, ma darlin.'

'Yes,' I says, 'an it's still hale.'

I had on a lovely white dress for it was midsummer, an the heavens opened an there was a rattle o thunder, a flash o lightnin an the rain began tae come doon.

'Stand under that tree,' he says, 'an I'll go back tae the hoose for your coat.'

I sheltered under the tree, wonderin tae masel if the auld bailer was still in the boat, that bailer that had got me intae sae much trouble. I went down to the boat an lookit in an there it was! I got intae the boat an went tae get the bailer, when ma feet slippit fae me again an I was oot like a light! Dead as a herrin!

When I came tae masel, it was dark wi stars shinin, but I could see nothin. I got the oars oot an I was pullin away an pullin away, first wi one oar, then the other, when ma arms began tae feel stronger. Soon I was goin lovely wi the two oars. Then I noticed a funny smell aff masel. Efter wearin new clothes ye notice that. It was a smell o sheep dip! I put ma hands on ma chest an it was as flat as a pancake. I had ma big auld jaicket on, ma troosers an ma big, auld, coorse, tackety boots.

'Oh,' I says, 'this is terrible. Oh ma man an ma bairns!'

Then I saw a light on the shore an I'm rowin like bleezes back. I reached the shore an there was ma lantern, still burnin! 'That must have been burnin a long time here!' I says. I took it in ma hand an went up the wee pad till I saw the light o the fairm. When I come in, there was the fairm just as I had left it, the samen hoose wi aa the company!

'Well,' says the fairmer, 'ye're back, Willie!'

'Aye,' I says, 'I'm back.'

'Did ye get the bailer?'

'There's your bailer,' I says. 'But you're never goin tae believe what's happened tae me.' An I telt the fairmer the story an he shook his heid. 'That would hae taken ye years tae do that, Willie,' he says.

'Oh aye,' I says, 'it took years. I've a wee boy o nine and anither o seven, an a husband.'

'Well,' says the fairmer, 'dae ye know how long ye were away? When you went oot it was twenty minutes tae twelve. Look at the clock noo.'

'It's twelve o'clock.'

'Well,' says the fairmer, 'when I asked ye tae tell a story, ye couldnae dae it at aa. Next time ye're asked tae tell a story, you'll have a story tae tell!'

Of course Willie had many a story to tell. Knowing him as I did, I regarded his habit of telling stories in the first person, as a technique designed to add impact, rather than a means of revealing autobiographical details. Although, I suppose you could say that a man who lives until he is ninety-one has had just about every experience it is possible to have!

Willie has often spoken about his travels in Ireland, whose songs he loved and where he sets some of his stories, like this one supposedly about himself as a young man. He did not give it a title but I always think of it as 'The Baby'.

The Baby

This happened tae me many many years ago. I'd had a row wi Bella ye see. Many years ago I was very quick tempered, but I've kind o cooled doon a bit noo. I'd had a row wi Bella and I thought I'd go off on ma ain track for a while and I went tae Ireland, ye see. There was nane o that fightin an blastin an daein hairm tae onybody back then in Ireland, sae I went away tae Ireland.

I cannae mind whether it was Belfast I arrived at or somewhere else, but when I cam aff the boat, it was getting dark as I started walkin oot thro the toon. I followed this dark narrow little road and it was lined on baith sides by high hedges. All of a sudden there was a great big peal o thunder and a heavy shower and I saiys, 'Oh this is a terrible shower!' There was a big deep drain at the side o the road sae I jumps doon intae it tae get a bit o shelter frae the rain. I got ma jaiket collar up roon ma neck like this. And tae tell the truth I wasnae that brave an I was kind o feart o the dark.

I heard footsteps comin doon the road an it was very very dark an I says, 'Oh there's heavy footsteps! Oh there's someone comin doon this way!' and ma heart started tae beat a bit. 'Well,' I says, 'I'll ask him the time or somethin', and as he cam alongside I could see the shape o the figure although it was very dark an I says, 'Hallo! Can ye tell me the time?'

'Oh my goodness!' says the figure. 'What did ye do that for? Ye've almaist frightened me oot o ma shoes!'

She says, 'An what are ye doin in there for, anyway, frightenin people like that?'

'Oh,' I says, 'I didnae mean ye ony hairm or anythin like that. I'm jist shelterin oot o the rain.'

'Ye're a Scotsman, aren't ye?'

'I am a Scotsman,' I says.

And she says, 'What are ye sittin in there for? Where are ye goin?'

I says, 'I don't know where tae go.'

She says, 'Come with me and I'll take ye tae a place. Do ye want some place for tae stay for the night?'

I says, 'That'll be fine!' And so we went away up the road and there was a wee village wi lights here and there. When we cam intae the light I could see she wis a nice-luikin young woman. She was a cracker ye know and I says, 'I've cracked it here tonight!'

'This is the place here,' she says. 'Ye'll get a bed here for the night and ye'll get some breakfast and maybe a cup o tea the night. But in the mornin afore ye go away, ye'll need tae split some sticks or somethin.'

'Oh that's all right. I'll certainly dae that!'

Now this house they came tae was a workhouse for the poor, you see. I chapped at the door but in the light I could see this woman was very fat but I wisnae that stupid and I says tae masel, 'I think this woman is goin tae hae a baby.' But when we came intae the light o this place I could see she was jist a young woman. Afore we went inside she says tae me, 'Look, I've been away from my husband for a while.'

I telt her that I had left ma wife and she said tae me, 'When we go in ye must say tae them and sign your name and say you are my husband. We'll maybe no get in if we're two strangers.'

'Oh that's okay,' I says and we go in. The man says, 'What dae ye want?'

I says, 'We're lost and got no place tae go wi a night's bed.'

He says, 'Oh ye can get a bed here all right. Just sign here. Whit's yer name?'

'Willie MacPhee,' I says, and I sign ma name in the book.

'What's yours?' he asks the woman.

'Oh I'm Mrs MacPhee,' she says. 'I'm Maggie MacPhee.'

'All right,' he says, 'Just sign there! Are you goin tae have a baby? This is no the time tae hae a baby, is it?'

'Naw, no really!' she says, 'but it's goin tae happen nevertheless.'

'Oh well,' says the man, 'ye'll hae tae hae that room aff that way.' Sae the woman is taken tae a room and I'm shown tae a separate room and I haed a guid sleep that night.

Aboot seven o'clock in the mornin I jist wakened up and this man cam in. He says, 'Come on! Get up! Get up!'

'Oh I'll get up all right!' I says.

He says, 'Ye'll be a proud man this mornin, MacPhee!'

'Why? Whit's happened?'

'Your wife had a lovely young son last night. Did ye no hear the sound o the bairn bein born?'

'No, I didnae hear a thing I slept that sound,' I says.

'Oh ye hiv a fine young son! Ye'll be a proud man this mornin!' he says.

'Ah well, ' I says, 'that's okay!'

He says, 'Well, ye cannae go away the day. Ye'll hae tae bide here three or four days till your wife's back on her feet.'

'Oh that's okay,' I says. 'It's no as if I've got anywhere tae go anyway.' Sae I stopped there for two or three days and soon the day cam that we had tae go out and the woman comes oot wi this lovely wee baby wrapped in a shawl, ye see. We thanked the man for everything he'd done for us.

'Well,' says the woman, 'that was very guid o ye tae tak the baby's name. Ye'll need tae come an we'll get it registered and sign the certificate,' she says.

'Well. Okay. I'll come wi ye then. So I gaes tae the Registrar's and I sign ma name and she signs her name and we come back up the wee village and there's a pub in it and we have a couple o shots.

She says, 'I'll tell ye what I'll do,' she says.'I have a wee bit o money. Would ye like a drink? Will ye take a pint o Guinness?'

I said, 'I wouldnae mind a pint o Guinness.'

So she orders a pint o Guinness fae the man.

'Where dae yez come fae?' says the ould man behind the bar. She explained tae him an he serves her wi two pints o Guinness. And so we were crackin away for aboot ten minutes then the wee baby started tae greet, ye see. And she says tae the man at the back o the bar, 'Have ye got any milk for the baby?'

'No, I've no milk, ' he says, 'The milk didnae come in yet.

But gin ye go tae the dairy in next door, you'll get some there.'

'Oh fair enough,' she says and she asks me tae haud the baby while she goes off next door.

'Of course I will,' I says, because I'm fair keen tae get a haud o the baby. So I takes a haud o this lovely wee baby boy and away she went for the milk. And I started rockin away back an forrit, cuddlin it in ma airms, and quietened it doon. I sat there waitin for its mither tae return for ten minutes, then fifteen minutes, then hauf an oor, still rockin the baby and there wis no sign o this woman comin back, ye see. I says, 'I wunner what's happened tae that woman, unless she's fell ill or somethin. Maybe she's fainted!' I says, tae the man at the bar, 'Will ye mind catchin this baby for a minute till I go and see what's happened tae the wife?'

'Aye,' he says. 'She shouldnae be that long away. It's just on the corner there, next door almost.'

So I gave the man the baby and the man took it ben and I gaed awa roon tae the dairy and gaed in. There's no sign o this woman, ye see. I asked. 'Was there a woman here a wee while ago for milk?'

'Naw, naw. There was never ony woman come in here,' says the dairy woman. 'I seen a woman but she wis goin awa doon the road at a hell of a lick, wherever she wis goin!'

'Whit? A big tall lassie?'

'Yes,' she says. 'She wis goin doon there like the wind, like the very Devil himself wis efter her.'

'Oh dear God! What am I goin tae dae now?'

Sae I wis goin back tae the pub when I suddenly said tae masel, 'Look, what's goin on here?' and I says, 'Naw, tae Hell wi this! I'm getting oot o here!' So I went away. Maybe aboot a week or so efter that I took a notion tae come back tae Scotland and I met back up wi Bella again.

It was aboot twenty year efter that and I had an auld caravan and we went tae Ireland on the same boat and we took the same road, ye see. And I says, 'This looks familiar. I wunner if this wee pub an this poorhoose is still there. Ah but there wis a lot o new hooses built by this time but this wee pub was still there and the wee dairy wis one o these multiple stores noo.

Bella says, 'Jist stop a minute and I'll go in one o these shops and I'll get somethin tae mak sandwiches and we'll get oor tea oot the road a wee bit.'

I says, 'Okay.' So I popped in tae the side o the road and I sat and looked at this wee pub and I remembered that's the wee pub I left the baby and thought aboot maybe goin in an havin a pint. I looked above the door and I seen ma name above the door, Willie MacPhee. 'Oh,' I says. 'I'll bet that's that young boy I left and these folk have left him the pub.'

So I come in tae the pub as bold as brass and standin at the back o the bar was this braw young man who was built like a hoose wi his shirt sleeves rolled up tae here. And he jist took one look at me and this is what he said tae me, 'I'm very sorry,' he says, 'we don't serve tinkers in here, so ye better get out or I'm goin tae get the Polis!'

I jist stood for a moment, and I looked at him. 'Well, well,' says I, 'it jist shows ye what some people is.'

But I never telt him what I'd done for him or nothin. Sae I jist walked back out again wi ma tail among ma feet. So that's ma story and I'm stickin tae it!

This apocryphal story might well have happened, not only to Willie but also to many other travellers in many different contexts. There is a song, written by a well-intentioned song-writer, which describes how Belle Stewart was supposedly turned away from a bar in Blairgowrie. But the idea is ludicrous.

If the bars in Blairgowrie had turned away travellers (especially one resident in the town all her life) they would have had to close! But this might well have happened elsewhere. Unlike 'The Bailer', this story has a ring of plausibility about it that teases the listener. We know he was no paragon of virtue in his youth and on that he bases the credibility of his story, which, of course, he swears is true.

The next story is also one of those Willie tells in the first person but that are not autobiographical. In his own words, he does it to make the story more convincing, because it is anything but. 'It sounds more like the thing if I tell it as if it happened to me.' This strange picaresque tale is supposed, again, to be about himself as a young man in Ireland.

A Tinker in Ireland

This was one time in Ireland with ma mother and faither and I was in my prime, about eighteen or so. At that time the trade was makkin tin an baskets and daein a wee job here and a wee job there. I got sick and tired of this and decided to go off on my own. I telt the old folk I wanted to get away for a spell so I gaithered up my tools and ma stake and aa the bits and pieces I needed for makkin tin an I traivelled the country luikin for an odd job. I likit a drink at that time, and I didnae like to drink too much aside the old people. I found work here an there mendin things wherever I could but ach! I got browned off wi this and I went intae Dublin one night and got drunk.

I was sittin away in a corner by myself when this darkie man come in. He sat doon in the ither corner. I was luikin at him an he was luikin at me but he was bolder an cam over an spoke tae me. 'I see,' he says, 'ye're a man like masel, ye like tae sit away ben the place, away fae the rest o the population.'

'Oh,' I says, 'I'm one of the travellin people. Ye've heard o the tinkers?'

'Oh yes,' he says, 'I've heard o the tinkers.'

'Well, I'm a tinker,' I says, 'an I dinnae like tae get mixed up wi ither people.'

'Well,' he says, 'I'm in the same boat as you. I dinnae like tae indulge in other people's affairs. I like tae drink by myself. But dae ye mind if I sit doon wi ye and have a drink?'

So him and I sat doon an cracked aboot — I dinnae mind it was that long ago. He asked me what I did for a livin. I telt him, 'I'm a tinker and I mak tin an mend things. But I gave that up an noo I'm luikin for a job.'

'Oh are ye?' he says. 'Did ye ever think aboot gaun tae sea?'

'Gaun tae see whit?' I says.

'I mean gaun tae sea in a boat?'

'Naw, naw,' I says. 'I was never at sea in ma life.'

'Well, I'm on a small boat. I'm the cook. An there was a boy used tae help me but he's gone away. We're luikin for someb'dy for his job. Jist tae gie me a hand in the galley tae cook for the people on the boat.'

'Whit wad I have tae dae?' I says.

'Oh ye'd have tae wash up the dishes an help me wi the pots an pans.'

'Oh I cuid dae that! How much pay wad I get for that?'

'Oh ye'd get good pay,' he says. Ye'll get aboot £10 to £15 pound and aa your food wad be free.'

'Oh that's aa right,' I says. 'Whaur is this boat noo?'

'It's doon at the harbour,' he says.

'That's aaright then,' I says. 'When will I see you?'

'Come in here the morn aboot ten o'clock. I'll see the captain an I'll bring ye on board aboot eleven o'clock.' I said that was okay.

So after that I got drunk and got my tools and my stake [a

small anvil on which tinsmithing can be done] and I went back on my tracks and gaed oot tae the end o the toon. I lay doon behind a hedge and fell soond asleep. But aboot five a.m. I woke and it was that cold, ma heid was sair and I was threatenin the bile. I lookit roon but couldnae see nothin. 'I'll need tae get back intae the toon tae meet this man.' So I hid ma tinsmithin tools under a wee brig. I cuid always come back and get them again whenever I needed them. When I went intae the toon the hotel was open all day so I went intae the bar. When it was ten o'clock the wee darkie man come in. 'Oh you're there,' he says. We had a drink an we went doon tae the pier. It was a big kin o coal boat aboot two hundred ton. And it carried coal back and forrit atween Scotland, Wales, England and Ireland. I met the captain and I says, 'This is my first time at sea and I dinnae ken much aboot it.'

'Oh,' he says, 'ye'll be all right, son. Sambo will show you the ropes,' he says. 'We're not goin very far this time. We're goin to Wales for a load o coal. Dinnae be afraid o the sea. There's no mony storms aboot here.'

So we went tae Wales and brought back the load o coal. Then we went further doon the English coast and brought back a load o lime.

After a couple o weeks I was startin tae enjoy masel. Everything was comin on lovely. But we went back, I think it was to Liverpool, and I remember we had tae bring back a load o machinery tae Ireland. Oh and it was a dark night when we set oot and a storm blew up wi wind and rain and it was ragin an ragin and the wind blew us clean aff oor course and we ran aground on rocks. The boat was breakin up and the captain shouted, 'Every man for himsel!'

Me and this darkie was together and we were friends so we jumped into the water together and we were aboot half a mile off the shore. I tried tae see the lights at a distance and it looked like a toon. We made for the shore and he was a strong swimmer and I was a strong swimmer tae. We managed to pull oorsels ontae it and we stayed there for aboot half an oor, pantin and shiverin wi cold and soakin wet, wi nothin on but oor troosers. 'Ah doot, MacPhee,' says the darkie, 'that we're finished.'

'Not at all,' I says, 'We'll be aa right.'

We seen the lights o cars goin back an forrit so we thought there was a road up there. We saw lorries comin doon an lorries gaun up and big lights. 'I think this must be an open-cast coal mine,' I says.

'I don't know what it is, man,' says the darkie.

We came roon a bend in the road an saw that it was this inorjurous [a word Willie often used for 'enormous'] big stane quarry wi lots o men workin overtime. There were lots o workmen's huts on every side o the road. 'Maybe there'll be an ould jaiket or somethin we cuid pit on to cover us,' I says. There was a big hut wi an open door and away at the back there was the blacksmith's shop o the quarry wi shafts and hammers and drills and picks. 'This is the very place,' I says, 'tae get a good heat.'

I gaithered sticks and pit them on the fire and we got a great blaze. 'Oh,' says the darkie, 'this is lovely!' The bellows was aboot this height above the grund and the darkie went in ablow the bellows and was doverin owre sleep. Then I'd blow the fire up again and worked the bellows and was doverin tae . . .

Then a whistle blew and all the work stopped. 'Whit's happenin noo?' I says. Aboot twenty men rushed into the hut and the gaffer came in and says, 'Whit's gaun on in here?'

'There's no much gaun on in here,' I says. 'I'm lost and I come in here for shelter.'

'Ye come in here for shelter?' he says. 'Fine story! Ye're a knockabout an a no good for nothin!'

'Naw naw!' I says, 'It's the truth I'm tellin ye. I'm no whit ye say I am. I cam in here for shelter.' He didnae believe me! So I says, 'Tae tell ye the truth, I'm a magician!'

'What?' he says.

'I'm a magician,' I says.

'Magician here, magician there!' says the gaffer. 'Ye're gaun tae get oot o here quick!'

'Are ye really a magician?' says anither man. 'Show us some o yer tricks!'

'Oh I can show ye a good trick,' I says, 'but ye might not like it!'

'If ye dinna show us a trick, yer body'll no go oot o here the nicht.'

I thocht tae masel, 'Whit am I gaun tae dae noo?' Then it struck me. I kent whit tae dae. The darkie was lyin ablow the bellows and they hadnae seen him. So I pit a wee lang iron into the fire til there wis sparks comin oot o it an it was rid hot. Then I shoved it unner the bellows up agen the darkie's back. God bliss me! The darkie come oot like a rabbit oot a hole, screamin – puir man, he didnae ken whit had happened – and the men thocht he was the Devil and ran for the door! The darkie took off for his livin life himsel.

After a few minutes the men aa came back in. 'Whit was that ye pit oot there?' they says.

'That wis the Devil,' I says. 'That's one o ma tricks. Dae ye want tae see ony mair?'

'Oh for God's sake, no, no,' they says. 'Nae mair tricks!'

They halved their tea wi me – it was a tea break – and one man gien me this jaiket, and I fun an auld pair o boots an pit them on. 'You jist bide here till the morn,' they says, 'then we'll see ye aa right.'

I thocht maybe the darkie wad come back an they'd fin oot I'm no a magician. 'I think I'd better get aff ma mark,' I says. I slippit oot as it was jist breakin daylicht and away doon the road. I fun it was the samen road whaur I'd hidden ma tools. I jumpit the dike and fun ma tools and ma stake and I gaed back tae ma ain job, mendin pots an pans up an doon the country.

I came doon this side road tae a wee smaa farm wi a shed. This auld wumman had a coo and a cuddy. 'Dae ye hae onythin tae mend?' I says.

'Oh yes,' she says. 'Ye're jist the man I was luikin for! I have this dish I milk ma coo intae an the milk's rinnin oot.'

I luikit an I seen the hole. 'Oh yes, granny,' I says. 'That's dead easy!' I mendit it an I says, 'I tell you what you can do afore ye do onythin else.'

'Whit's that?' she says.

'I had nae breakfast the day, granny,' I says, 'sae if you can gie me a cup o tea, that'll be the payment for the dish.'

'That's very nice of you,' she says. She made me a good breakfast wi twa duck eggs, a bit fried ham, a great big floury scone fried in the gravy and a big bowl o tea.

'Dae ye live here aa by yersel?' I says.

'Yes,' she says. 'Ma son has learned tae be a doctor in Dublin. I haven't seen him for four months.'

'Ye've got a nice wee place here,' I says. Then I took ma leave o her and gaed on ma way.

I buggered aboot for a bit, daein a job here and a job there and made a few shillin. Then I gaed back intae Dublin and I got drunk as usual. I was stotterin oot the road again when this big motor overtook me. It stopped. 'There's one o them,' said someb'dy in the car. One o them came oot o this door and one o them came oot o that doot and they made a dive at me. But I was too smart. I dropped everything and jumped the dike and run away. But everywhere I run this big motor was afore me. They scanned their lights across the fields and luikit for me.

But I run doon the side o this wood and up the back o this hedge, and here I cam tae the samen wee cottage where I mended the auld wumman's dish.

'Oh I'll get in here,' I says and I went up an chappit on the door.

'Who's there?' says this voice.

'It's me, granny,' I says. 'I'm the man who mended your dish. I'm bein chased by men and I don't know why.'

'Jist open the door tae the byre and slip in there,' she says. 'You go in there wi the coo on the top o the hay,' she says.

'Fair enough,' I says. I slippit in the door o the byre and there was this thing built above the coo's stall, like a rack for the hay tae feed the beast. I got up in there and droppit ma boots aff an they fell intae the coo's trough. Then I lay doon and fell asleep.

But then I heard the car again and men come in the door and one o them says, 'He micht be in here. He cannae be far awa.'

Then I kent what it was aboot!

So I got up tae the tap and oot by this skylight windae. I heard whit they were sayin.

'He's no here,' he says. 'But jist look at that! There his boots!' he says. 'The coo must have ett him and left nothin but his boots!'

An that's the last that I saw o them!

There are two interesting features of this story. One is that the ending is similar to that of 'The Wandering Piper', which reveals something of the storymaker's art and the existence of motifs that can be used in different stories. The comic effect of 'the coo must have ett him' is if anything even more hilarious than in the story of the piper. The other feature is that although Willie tells us beforehand that the story is not really about himself, everything in the story is within his own experience and the character reacts to situations very much as Willie himself might have done. Willie had a 'stake', or small anvil, along with tinsmithing tools including tinsnips, soldering irons and hacksaws, like the young man in the story, and he also had the knowledge and experience to use them. Hiding them in the undergrowth under a little bridge with the idea that he could find them there again when he needed them, shows how the travellers thought of themselves as belonging to the countryside; 'we own the world's room', as Adam MacNaughtan's song puts it. Willie was also used to looking for work and taking whatever chance presented itself, whether it was something he had done before or not. The meeting in the Dublin pub between the young man and the 'darkie' is an interesting situation that seems to feature two marginalised individuals. The implication is that society is prejudiced against both of them, but also that they both like their privacy, an idea that does not occur to those who exclude them. This is what draws them to each other.

However, for those within the travelling culture, life could offer many benefits. One of the things Willie enjoyed was the variety it could offer. Particularly as a young man, he would become 'browned off' with one job and quickly find something else because he was willing to turn his hand to anything. This gives a lively example of the traveller's survival skills.

Lashed by the storm, the boat sank and the two struggled ashore, showing how in a disaster it is the humanity of the people involved that is important, not their race or social class. The supposed raising of the Devil in the workman's hut in the quarry seems a curious contrast to the note of common humanity that has been struck when the two men helped each other ashore. Certainly the young man is in a tight corner and has to take drastic action to reassert his control of the situation. Having claimed to be a magician, which many travellers are thought to be, he has to do 'a magic trick' and chooses to do something that shows little regard for the 'darkie': in fact it causes him excruciating pain. This has the effect of restoring the workmen's trust in him. It is only when he thinks of the consequences of his actions that he realises the situation is still dangerous for him. When he runs out he finds himself near where he hid his tools. As fortune turns the wheel, the young man reverts to his tinsmithing, as the mysterious 'big, black car', reminiscent of the Burkers (bodysnatchers), brings in the shadow of the 'civilised world'. We never know if the men who are on the hunt for him are police, or political thugs. They are the outsiders, who prey on the travellers, for whatever reason, and whom the travellers feared. This rather unlikely and amusing story gives us a good insight into the outlook on the vagaries of life that travellers have.

6 The Supernatural

Most travellers believe in the supernatural, although, with many of them, that translates into a kind of spirituality and recognition of a higher power that with some could have a Christian form. Certainly, as Louise Hay observed, many of them read the Bible and regarded religion as a private matter that had little to do with church-going. Belle Stewart told me that the first thing a new mother and father hastened to do was register the birth of their child, then visit the minister and have the baby christened. The fact that the minister would hansel the child with a half crown may have had some bearing on this. But it was more likely that the existence of the Burkers, or bodysnatchers, would encourage them to make the birth official. Some travellers were married in a church or by a minister, and they certainly wanted a minister to officiate at a funeral. Many, however, seemed to follow the old Scots custom of hand-fasting, having families and staying together for many years, often until the death of one of them. How much more married can you get? Most ministers in country parishes understood this and seldom refused to marry or bury anyone. There were exceptions of course – like the Blairgowrie minister who refused to bury Alec Stewart in 1980 and spoke of him as 'one of those people' – but there were also ministers like the one from Alyth who was proud to officiate at Alec's funeral. He regarded him with great respect and affection, although he had never met him. The family could avoid all difficulty over the burial of Belle in 1998 because by that time her grandson Hamish was a minister. Willie's funeral took place in a little country church at Gartocharn; the service was given by a benevolent minister who must have known Willie's family and been known to them.

The northern travellers were no different from other Highlanders in believing in the supernatural. Gaelic culture abounds in all kinds of spirits and entities, some of which take the form of ghosts and witches, though often these latter are regarded simply as wise old women and wise old men. Haunted places were often featured in stories and people anxious to avoid trouble would avoid such areas. In Willie's case, he grew up with stories of wee men in green, haunted places and magic objects that threw up thorny forests and stormy seas. While he may have believed them when he was young, as he grew older he learned to use these supernatural apparitions with strange powers as tools of the imagination in storytelling. Knowing him for more than forty years, I was not aware that his life was affected by superstition to the extent that those of some other travellers were. But there is hardly a story he told that did not have a supernatural element in it, whether it be a witch or a warlock, the Devil himself, some magical shape-shifting or a spell of some kind that can only be undone by some magic procedure.

I have heard tales of travellers gathered together (perhaps for safety, but motivated by curiosity) in order to see whether the tale about the White Lady of Ardrishaig was true. Certainly I have been told to go to a burial ground on Loch Aweside to see proof of the skeleton rising from the grave and striking the wall above the head of the wee cripple tailor who got back the use of his legs from the fright he was given. Willie's stories take for granted that listeners either believe or practise 'a willing suspension of disbelief' when following stories.

Stories, the wisdom of the past and the knowledge needed to help one deal with negative emotions like fear and hatred, and problems one encountered in life's journey, give the traveller's storytelling repertoire a relevance and a depth. This has been lost nowadays by people who make the mistake of regarding storytelling as an amusement for children. Like the travellers from whom I have learned so much, I have been all over Scotland telling stories and singing songs to schools and local groups. My recordings were made in my friends' homes, with a mixed family group sitting around, of all ages. Nowadays a storyteller is faced by groups all of the same age: children, old people (many of whom can tell stories of their own lives) mothers and toddlers, students, and so on. Adults, even parents, avoid these events if they possibly can.

Fortunately I have seen Willie at work, telling stories to groups of old and young, sometimes with plenty of time, sometimes with just a half-hour 'slot.' He just took whatever came and lengthened or shortened his stories as required. He also suited the way he told the story to the people who were listening. After all, he was used to holding the attention of a large group of people and to him any human group had to be spoken to appropriately and perhaps on different levels, just as a story may be enjoyed by old and young, male or female, kinfolk or strangers. Travellers learned a long time ago in their dealing with the public how to talk to people in such a way that they will listen. Anyone who tries to do something that looks easy and effortless often has an eye-opening experience. One may think that nowadays children are familiar with the world of the imagination because of the popularity of so-called 'magic' fantasies. But the really 'magic' stories are those that help the listeners realise their own potential and cope with their personal difficulties. These listeners are supported by the older folk through family solidarity and a feeling of community, both of which have declined in the modern social scene. Young and old like stories, particularly when they are 'told', not recited from memory as if learned from a book. My storytellers, like Willie, learned their stories in their family circle or in the course of their social life, by hearing them again and again. Willie knew that if he visited a school or a festival it was a one-off. But he was a believer in the spiritual value of his tales, as he made clear in stories like 'Johnny Pay Me for My Story'.

Willie also knew about the 'magic' of knowledge, and the control it gave people who were enabled by it to do things they could not do before. There were many legends about pipers and Willie knew most of them. He had a particularly imaginative view about how pipe tunes were passed on, setting more store by supernatural tales than by tunes in books. After all, that is how he learned a great many tunes before he amazingly taught himself to read bagpipe music (which suggests that he could have become literate if the circumstances of his early life had allowed it). But then he might have had his memory and command of words influenced by schooling and lost the freedom that the oral tradition gave him. The reason he could learn tunes and songs by hearing them was, of course, because he had a good ear and a good memory, but to him that was a kind of magic and it is hard not to consider it so. In the setting of the Highland landscape, where the travellers camped in tents or trailers, one can easily imagine a man lying in his bed, out of the elements and the mysterious dark, and hearing the distant sound of piping. It is even possible to hear the same tune being *cainntearachd* (a method of passing on tunes in which the piper sings syllables that tell what notes are to be played and how) within earshot of the listener. Perhaps that is the explanation behind the stories of pipers receiving tunes from the fairies. Both Willie and Alec had a story about how they learned the tune they called 'The Ghost Piper of Ballachulish'. A man lying dovering in his trailer 'up the glen' hears a piper playing a tune that is new to him and is able to reproduce it. This sounds plausible and, to the recipient, it has come about through the magic of hearing it without seeing the piper's face or fingers, so the piper is thought of as a 'ghost'. Certainly the surroundings help to suggest the idea of the supernatural source. But to Willie the real magic lay in the music and the ability of pipers to create it.

Ghosts are an interesting phenomenon in the travellers' belief system. I have never thought it useful to establish whether a ghost story is true or not, in the literal sense. Judgment of such situations is very subjective and if it is true to the person it happens to, then it is true. In the case of people generally, belief in ghosts is born of a desire to have those we have lost returned, but it is worth remarking that ghosts are also feared. Perhaps it is because they are not natural that they seem to come from another world and belong to a different mode of existence. At any rate it is something we do not understand. Also, travellers would not be inclined to question this magical notion. To men like Willie, the world is full of wonders and the otherworld is very real and very close at hand. It is noticeable that 'fairy' tunes are not feared but welcomed and regarded as a gift. One has also to remember the survival instincts of the traveller that teach him to use every bit of luck that comes his way.

Another ghost story in Willie's repertoire is of the Grey Lady at the Beech Hedges of Meikleour, whom he saw dressed in a ballgown when passing there one night. There was another Lady of Ardrishaig that he also saw, which prompts the question, are the psychically aware people, who believe in apparitions, more likely to see them than the more sceptical? It has to be pointed out that he saw the Lady at Ardrishaig when a large number of travellers gathered there together to test the existence of the ghost. They wanted to believe in it, but their common sense told them they needed proof. They had clearly not heard of group hysteria.

An example of a story that Willie learned from another storyteller, Duncan Williamson, and told in his own way was 'The Devil's Money'. There are quite a lot of tales of trickery involving the Devil and a game. The idea of games of skill is a popular one in many human groups. Also, there is a suggestion of disreputable excitement about a game that involves risk of any kind. But travellers are born risk-takers and Willie was no exception, which is probably why he liked the story. In addition to that, finding money lying on the ground would tempt anyone.

The Devil's Money

There was once an auld wumman an she lived wi her son an och! she was a frail auld body. Noo and then she used tae send her son tae the shop, an he was a drunken sot. Every time he went tae the shop he had tae get maybe five or six shillings tae get himsel a drink afore he would come back. He had aboot five mile tae walk doon the road, but if crossed by this near-cut he'd only aboot two miles.

This day, onywey, it comes his turn tae go to the shop. 'Well,' says his mother, 'laddie, I'm tellin ye, don't come back that near-cut. Come right roon the road and never come through a near-cut in the dark.'

'Ach,' he says, 'it'll be aa richt, mither. Nothin'll touch me!'

'Well,' she says, 'please yersel.'

Away he went tae the shop and when he had got his shoppin, he went intae the pub wi the rest o the money an got drunk. He's comin back and, 'Ach,' he says, 'I'm no travellin roon that road. I'll be hame in half the time if I could cross this near-cut.'

So he's comin across by this near-cut and the mune's shinin clear an he luckit an saw this thing shinin on the ground. 'I wonder what that is?' he says. He bent doon an liftit it an it was a sovereign! 'Where did that come fae?' he says. 'O wish I had come this road in the daylicht. I would hae found this sovereign an I would be a lot drunker gaun hame!'

He come alang another wee bit an he saw anither yin shinin an he pickit it up tae. He went alang yairds an yairds an he's funnin these sovereigns as he gaed alang till he had aboot a dizzen o these sovereigns. Aa o a sudden these sovereigns took a bend aff the path away up tae this wood an he's pickin an odd yin here and an odd yin there an he comes tae this cave. He stoppit at the door o this cave an luckit an he saw a light away inside like the light o a fire. 'Oh this must be some auld tramp that's in here,' he says. 'He must hae robbit some place an that was money that fell oot o his bag. I'll go in here an see him.'

So he comes away intae the end o this cave an this was the Devil sittin wi a fire. 'Aha,' he says. 'You're here, Jeck.'

'Aye, I'm here,' he says.

The Devil says, 'How did ye get up here?'

'I follaed a trail o money,' he says.

'Oh ye did?' he says. 'You're a bad lad, ye know. Every shillin your mother had, ye've drinkit, spendin it an wastin it. That was you the nicht, doin the same thing.'

'Ach well,' he says, 'it's nae business o yours whit I dae.'

'Oh,' he says, 'it's my business aa richt. It's up tae me aa richt, for I'm gaun tae get ye in the lang run.'

'I don't think so,' says Jeck. 'I don't think so.'

As he sat crackin wi the Devil, he says, 'How much money did ye get, Jeck?'

'Oh I got a lot o money.'

'Let's see't.'

Jeck pit his hand in his pocket an when he pulled it oot it was a handfu o earth he had! The Devil says, 'Ye've nae money noo. That's for bein bad. But I tell ye what. There a box o gold sovereigns lyin there. I'll gie ye as mony gold sovereigns as ye can carry, if ye can bate me.'

'Bate you?' he says. 'Maybe I could bate you an maybe I couldnae.'

'Well,' says the Devil, 'it's genuine money. If ye can bate me, takin it oot, ye can have it!'

Jeck saw the cloven hoof on the Devil. Noo, he was that lazy when he was in his mother's hoose, if his mither telt him tae put a bit stick or a bit peat on the fire, instead o usin his hands, he wad lift the end o the stick or the peat wi his fit an pit it on the fire.

'Well, Jeck,' says the Devil, 'Whit are ye gonnae dae? It's up tae you.'

'If I can tak the money oot,' says Jeck, 'some wey that you cannae tak it oot. Will ye gie me't?'

'The Devil's in command,' he says. 'On ye go!'

So he took aff his shoe, pit his fit intae the box an liftit a guid puckle siller. 'Now,' says Jeck. 'Can you dae that?'

'Aye,' says the Devil, 'I can dae that!' But o coorse the Devil could lift naethin wi his cloven fit an he went away in a flash o fire.

When Jeck came to he was lyin ootside the cave an he still had this heap o money aside him. 'Well,' he says, 'that was funny. I've never seen the Devil afore.' He liftit the money and pit it in his pocket and came batterin hame tae his mither.

'Well,' she says, 'you're back!'

'Aye,' he says, 'I'm back!'

'Did ye come the near-cut?'

'Aye,' he says.

'It's a wonder ye didnae see the Devil on that road,' she says.

'Aye, but I did see him. I saw the Devil on that near-cut!'

'Well,' she says, 'it's a wonder ye're here!'

'I saw the Devil an I bate the Devil.' Jeck says.

'How did ye bate him?'

'I made him lift money oot o a box wi his fit an he couldnae, wi his cloven fit!' he says.

'Ah, ye're mad!' she says.

'There's the gold,' he says. 'The Devil's money!'

An it kept them gaun for a lang, lang time!'

The travellers' belief in something beyond the material world has a strong influence on their way of life, their attitude to other people and the value they attach to abstractions like love and hate, wisdom and folly and even life and death.

'Johnny Pay Me for My Story' is full of supernatural beliefs that show the close relation between the traveller's life and the spiritual otherworld. The idea of human beings being able to learn from the world of nature and acquire strength, mobility and cunning from the lion, the salmon and the hawk, also gives him mastery of the elements of earth, water and air. At the same time, he has to learn to value this without arrogance or selfishness. In Willie's story, the source of wisdom is unequivocally God. The other boy, who gives the old storyteller the right answer to his demand for payment, says, 'I can't pay you, but maybe God'll pay you,' is seen to have spiritual insight. This is what Johnny learns from his experiences. The storyteller is also the bearer of wisdom, but it is one thing knowing something in theory and quite another putting it in to practice. That is what Johnny does in the second part of the story for his own benefit. He uses the physical gifts of strength, speed and cleverness to become capable of heroism. Then comes the third part of the story, which is almost entirely supernatural. 'The Giant Whose Heart is in an Egg' is a motif found worldwide in folklore. If he seeks out and destroys the egg, he destroys the giant. He also incidentally rescues a princess in thrall to him.

This next story can be used to illustrate the importance of ties of kinship in life but is is also a supernatural story and linked to the idea of wish fulfilment.

The Beard

Once upon a time there was an old man and an old woman lived on the edge of a big forest and they had three sons. Things got so bad on their wee small croft that the family had to go away and look for work for theirsels. The eldest says, 'I think, boys, we'll go away and look for a job for wursels and let the old folks bide here till we come back and we'll bring them some money back.'

'A good idea,' said the second brother. 'We'll do just that.'

They packed up and away they went and they traivelt many miles and it startit getting dark. The oldest brother says, 'I think the best thing we can dae, boys, is get off the road a bit, intae the shelter o the wood and kennle a fire and put up there for the night.'

Away they went intae the wood and kennlet a fire, had a sup o something and lay doon. Very early next mornin they wakent up and there wis sic a thick mass o trees roon aboot them, they didnae ken whit direction they'd come or whit direction they had tae go. So they set in through this wood and traivelt on and on and on an the further they were goin the thicker it was gettin and they couldnae get back ontae the road again. They were that tired they couldnae go ony further, so the auldest yin says, 'You sit there, boys, and kennle a fire an I'll see the reek fae a distance. I'll go an see if I can find the road again.'

The ither two kennlet a fire an they're sittin an it was two hours when he finally came back. 'I don't know where the road is,' he says, 'but I came across a nice wee hut. We could pass the night there.'

When they cam to the hut there was a table and chairs, a big bed and plenty o meat in the presses. 'There must be someb'dy bidin here.' the auldest yin says. They made theirsels a tichtener-up [a meal, which 'tichtens up' the stomach] and they spent the night there. The auldest brither says, 'We're as well stoppin here as gaun any farther. We can trap an get some skins an that'll make good money.'

The ithers says, 'We'll jist dae that.'

'Now John,' says the auldest yin, 'ye're the youngest so you can stop an watch the hut the day till we go away huntin, an hae oor supper ready when we come back.'

So John bidit in the hut an away the two went. John's cookin this big pot fu o meat, a big potfu o tatties an a big potfu o soup. He's stirrin the pot an singin away when a chap comes tae the door.

'Oh,' he says, 'that'll be the boys back. I better open the door tae them.' He opens the door and looks oot. This was a wee man, jist knee-high.

'Hallo,' says the wee man.

'Hallo,' says John. 'Are you the man belongin tae this hut?'

'Oh no, no,' says the wee man. 'This is no ma hut. But I'm very hungry. I could dae wi somethin tae eat.'

'Oh,' says John, 'come away in! Plenty here for everybody!'

So the wee man came in and John fillt a big basin tae him and gien him that. Oh the wee man was away wi it in seconds!

'That wis good,' he says, 'John, I could dae wi a bit more!'

'Oh,' says John, 'ye'll get some more!' John gien him the

second helpin and in seconds, it's away again! Says John, 'Ye can fairly eat, wee man, tae be a wee man!'

'Oh I can eat,' he says, 'and I want some more off ye!'

'Well, I'll give ye a wee drop,' says John, 'but I've just got enough for my brothers after that. Ye cannae get ony mair.'

'Ye better gie me some more,' says the wee man, 'or it'll be the worse for ye!'

'Ye'd better slip yersel,' says John, 'afore I gie ye a good kickin oot the door.'

'Oh ye think ye can gie *me* a kickin?' says the wee man.

'Aye,' says John. 'I think I could!' He's a big strong young man and this man's only knee-high. But he wouldnae go.

'Are ye gaun tae gie me the rest o the meat that's in the pot, or am I gaun tae take it oot o yer hide?'

John says, 'Ye're no getting it!'

The wee man startit on him and John's punchin him here and there but he's no daein onythin tae the wee man. Then the wee man startit, heid doon, and near endit John's life, brak every bane in his body and he's lyin oot for the count and the wee man ate everythin that was lyin. John's lyin in a corner murnin and the bluid's comin oot o him when a chap comes tae the door again. 'Oh,' he says. 'There he's comin back again! He's comin tae kill me this time!' But it was his brothers back and yin o them had a deer across his back and the ither yin had a couple o foxes. 'What happened tae ye?' says the auldest brother. 'Whit are ye daein lyin in a corner? Where's oor supper?'

'I had a good supper waitin on yese,' he says, 'an there was a wee man come tae the door an I gien him half o what was there. He nearly endit ma days an he's away wi the lot!'

'Ah,' says the second brother, 'John must hae suppit the lot an he went an fell against the stanes jist tae let on!'

'I'm tellin you,' says John, 'that wee man wad kill the three o us!'

'Well,' says Geordie, the second brother, 'he'll need tae kill me, the morn. You gae oot an hunt wi Willie, and I'll wait an see whit happens!'

Samen thing happened again. The second brother had these pots boilin fu o meat and soup an back comes this wee man again. Geordie says, 'Were you here yesterday?'

'Aye,' says the wee man.

'Were you the man that ate oor meat?'

'Oh I never ate much,' he says. 'I just got a wee drap fae yer brother.'

'An what dae ye want noo?' says Geordie.

'I want ma dinner!'

'O come in,' says Geordie, 'an get some dinner.'

Poor Geordie didnae ken whit was gaun tae happen tae him! The wee man came in and Geordie gien him a bowl o soup and a big plate o meat an tatties. Aw jist in seconds, it was away! Second helpin – away in seconds! Third helpin, seconds – away!

The wee man says, 'Gie me the rest!'

'Aw,' says Geordie, 'ye cannae have the rest!'

The wee man said, 'I'm gaun tae dae the same wi you as I did wi your brother.'

'Well,' said Geordie, 'ye managed him, but I'm a bit aulder an a bit bigger. I doot I'll gie ye a tougher faa.'

This wee man startit tae Geordie, an if he gien the younger brother a beatin, he gien Geordie a worse yin. He nearly killt him aathegither.

The ither two came back fae huntin an Willie, the aulder brother, lookit in an says, 'Did that wee man get you tae?'

Geordie says, 'He's no human!'

Next day, Willie says, 'I'll wait the day an see this wee man when he comes.'

Willie's left wi this big potfu o soup, a pot o tatties, a pot o beef, lovely and tasty, when the chap comes tae the door again. Willie goes tae the door and looks. 'Oh it's you,' he says.

'Aye,' says the wee man, 'it's me.'

'You were here yesterday,' says Willie, 'and you were here the day before.

'That's right,' says the wee man.'

Willie says, 'You ate wir dinner yesterday an the day before yesterday.'

'That's right,' says the wee man, 'an I'm gaun tae eat yours today and I'm gaun tae sort ye oot tae.'

'Oh I doot, I doot,' says Willie, 'ye couldnae dae that. I'm a bigger man than the other two and I'm strong!'

So the wee man come in an Willie fillt a great bowl wi soup an gien him it an a great lot o tatties an a great lump o beef. He soon put this lot doon an Willie says, 'Are ye wantin more?'

'I want some more,' says the wee man. Gien him a second issue.

'Are ye wantin more?'

More again!

He gien him an gien him till he had gien him the lot. This wee man had a belly on him! But there was drainins left in the pot an he says, 'Gie me the rest o that!'

'Oh,' says Willie, 'ye've had your share and ye're no getting ony mair!'

'Well,' says the wee man, 'if ye're no gaun tae gie me that, ye better get your jacket off and see whit ye can dae.'

So the wee man started but by good luck the ither two brothers didnae go so very far away this day an they came back early. The three o them set aboot this wee man and Willie made a grab and got a haud o his baird wi his two hands an the ither two's kickin him.

'Oh,' says the wee man, 'I've had enough! I've had enough! Let go ma baird!'

'Naw,' says Willie, 'ye're no getting away. I have ye cockled when I've got ye by the baird!'

'For ony sakes,' says the wee man, 'I'll gie ye onythin in the world, if ye'll let go ma baird!'

'I'll pull it off by the root!' says Willie.

The wee man says, 'I'll gie ye gold an I'll gie ye silver, as much as ye can cairry away, an diamonds and rubies, if ye'll let go ma baird!'

'No,' says Willie, 'I'm no lettin go!'

The wee man says, 'I'll show ye where there is a castle an young ladies tae your will, an jewels and diamonds, if ye'll let go ma baird!'

'No,' says Willie, 'I'm takkin your baird aff,' an he rippit the beard aff an the wee man's rinnin aboot wi plooks o watter whaur the baird was. The wee man says, 'For God's sake, gie me ma baird back again!'

'I'm haudin on tae this baird,' says Willie, 'till ye tell me whaur aa this gold is.'

'I'll show ye whaur it is,' says the wee man.

Willie says, 'What aboot the baird, that it's sae precious?'

'Well,' says the wee man, 'that's a magic baird, and wherever ye want tae go an whatever ye want tae dae, say three words tae that baird an ye land there.'

'Well, first,' says Willie, 'ye better show me where the ladies are, an this castle ye've been tellin me aboot.'

Away the wee man walks alang this nerra pad through this wood till he comes tae this huge beech tree wi a big hole in it.

'Noo,' says the wee man, 'that's where ye get everything ye want, doon in that tree.'

'You go doon first,' says Willie, 'and I'll follae ye doon.'

The wee man went doon intae the hole, right away under the ground. The three o them follaed him an they traivelt doon this passage till it broke back oot intae a valley an there was the loveliest castle ye ever saw in your life.

'There's the castle,' says the wee man, 'There's plenty o money and plenty o everything there, an there are ladies there too, if ye want to go in.'

'Go ahead,' says Willie.

'I'm feart tae go in,' says the wee man.

'How are ye feart?' says Willie.

'I put them in there,' says the wee man. 'I stole them but they have no power on me because o that baird. That's the whole secret o the thing.'

'What have I tae dae wi the baird?' says Willie.

'There's some magic words,' says the wee man. 'Three professors in ma baird. I wish I was – wherever ye want tae be!'

'Oh is that it?' says Willie. 'Well, up ye go tae the castle till we see what's there.'

Up went the wee man an he's fair shakin wi fricht an whenever he opened the door o the castle there were these three young ladies an they had nae power tae come oot through the door. The three brothers went roon aa the rooms tae see what was in them an they were packit wi jewels. Willie says, 'I better fill a bag wi these jewels!'

So they filled the bag wi the gold and diamonds an each o them took one o these lassies by the hand an Willie lifted the baird an says, 'Three professors in ma baird, I wish the six o us were back home!'

Wheech! Like a flash they were standin back home at the door o their own place. Their father lookit at them. 'Wait a minute, boys,' he says, 'what's this?'

Willie telt him whit happened and how the wee man nearly endit their days an then showed them where the jewels were.

'Oh,' says the old man, 'an how did ye manage tae get back here?'

Willie telt him. 'Whitever ye say tae this baird it happens.'

'Oh is that right?' says the auld man. 'Whit is it ye say?'

'Ye jist say,' says Willie, '"Three professors in ma baird, I wish I was in – some place." Ye see?'

The auld man catches the baird an says, 'Three professors in ma baird, I wish me an ma wife was in that valley where the boys were.'

The auld man an his wife disappeared an if they went tae that valley, they're still in that valley yet!

When the brothers in the story leave home to seek their fortune, they are in the frame of mind to make the best of whatever they encounter, and to use the solidarity of their brotherhood to do so. The number three is almost a magical number in folktales, in which we find three brothers, or sisters, three tasks, three markets, three riddles, and so on. Willie always said of unusual or unexpected events, whether happy or sad, easy or difficult, hurtful or comforting, that things went in threes, and particularly if there had been two of these that there would be a third. In this story it is the oldest and strongest brother that puts them in the position of acquiring the beard, which is their key to good fortune. The end of the story about 'The Beard' also suggests that sons share their good fortune with their parents. They go out in to the world to see what they can do, but they do not forget those they have left behind.

As well as stories that provided a template for personal development, there were stories about life on the road. Luck and chance played a big part in the survival of the travelling people and wish fulfilment also helped to shape the stories that were told, like Willie's version of 'The Three-fittit Pot'.

The Three-fittit Pot

Once upon a time there was a traveller man and a traveller woman. They had naethin in the world. But he was a peaceful-livin man, he never did any harm, never was in jail, he jist lived tae traivel roon the countryside wi his wife and twa weans. He could make baskets and tin, play the pipes, sing songs and he was a great man for throwin the stane and playin quoits, a great sportsman. An it was a hard time wi them.

They're traivellin away up this back glen and they hadnae as much as wad make tea tae theirsels an the weans were gaspin wi hunger. He made twa baskets wi green wands – he never peeled them – an he says tae his wife, 'If ye can sell thae twa baskets, we could maybe get somethin. God knows whether there's a shop.'

'Well,' she says, 'I'll try ma best.' They came up this road and there was a bit o a fairm. 'Try,' he says, 'if there's a man there at aa, an ask him if he's a bit o tobacco. I'm dyin for a smoke!'

The woman goes tae the fairm an raps at the door an oot comes this big tall woman. 'What dae ye want?' she says.

'I've twa wee weans doon there,' says the traveller woman, 'an ma man. We're dyin o starvation.'

'Oh dear,' says the woman. 'That's no sae guid. What's that ye've got there?'

'That's two baskets, mistress,' says the traveller woman.

'That's the very thing I need tae gaither ma eggs. Come away in an I'll gie ye somethin for the weans an yersel.' She took her intae the kitchen o the fairm an it was spotless and beautiful. She gien her tea and sugar, milk and scones and meal, a puckle o flooer and a big lump o ham. 'If ye wait till ma man comes in, I'll gie ye a puckle tatties.'

'Oh,' says the traveller woman, 'that's fine. I'll tell ye wan thing. Ma man's never had a smoke for days, an he's dyin for a smoke.'

'Oh,' says the woman, 'I'll gie ye a smoke.' An she went tae a caddy on the mantelpiece and gien the woman a lump o tobacco.

'Aw, thanks very much, ma'am,' says the traveller woman.

'Where are ye gaun tonight?' asks the farmer woman.

'Oh we'll go up the glen an maybe get a place tae stop,' she says.

'If ye go up there,' says the farmer woman, 'there an auld wastins that was wan o the plooman's hooses an it tumblet doon. Ye'll get strae for your bed an ye can bide there as long as ye like.'

'Thanks very much,' says the woman. She went doon the road and telt her man this an they went up an fund this wastins an pit up their tent. 'Whit a beautiful place for the tent,' he says, 'wi clean watter an everythin runnin by there.'

'Now, says the woman,' we've nae dishes. If I had ony kin o pot I could boil these tatties.'

'Aye,' says the man, 'that's richt.' An he's away roon the auld hoose, an the cupboards are still there belonging tae the folk an there was naethin in them till he cam tae wan an there was a three-fittit pot in it, beautiful and clean, jist like a shillin inside.

'That's the very thing,' she says, an she took it tae the burn an scourt it clean wi a sod. Then she boiled the tatties in it. 'Thank God for that pot,' she says, 'a thing I was needin aa ma days.' She washed it clean an pit it upside doon on the top o their barra an they went tae their beds.

They were lyin in their bed maybe a couple o oors when they heard a rummle ootside. She says, 'Hey, man, hey!'

'Whit is it?' he says.

'There's somethin oot there tryin tae steal ma pot!'

'Awa!' he says. 'Ye're mad! Wha wad come trailin up the glen tae steal *your* pot?'

They fell soun asleep again. The pot got off the barra, away up the road tae the big hoose! Next day there was goin tae be a big shoot an the chef was makin a dinner for aa these gillies an things, wi partridges, pheasants an hens and this great inorjurous roast. The pot goes in to the kitchen where the chef was workin. 'I wonder,' he says, 'where I could put this roasted leg o mutton?' He looks an he sees the pot an he says, 'The very thing!' He pits the leg o mutton intae't an goes away tae his bed.

Doon the pot came tae the road an tae where the barra was. Next day when she got up the woman lookit for her pot. 'Aw,' she says, 'hey, man! Come tae ye see whit's in the pot!' This was the roasted leg o mutton. 'Maybe the woman on the fairm took pity on us and cam doon an left this for the weans!'

'Oh,' he says, 'that's what it must hae been!'

That nicht, the woman boiled mair tatties in her pot and they ate them tae the leg o mutton. Then she washed the pot again and put it on top o the barra and they went tae their bed again. They're jist sleepin when the pot goes off on its three legs and and makes for the castle. It goes in the back door and up the lobby tae where the ould gentleman o the castle is sittin at a table countin his money. Sovereigns and half-sovereigns and gold trinkets! He's lookin for a place tae pit them in when he's counted them and he sees the pot. 'Aw, jist a fine thing,' he says, 'tae haud ma money!' An he's in wi the sovereigns intae the pot an he rises tae go away for somethin else and the pot struggles oot the door an back tae the tent.

When the man an wumman got up in the mornin an the man went tae the pot tae look at it, he nearly faintit! He gien a roar an held his hairt. 'Jeannie, come here tae ye see this! We're quoddit! We're quoddit!'

'What is it, Jack?' she says.

'The pot's hauf full o lour!'

They endit up arguin aboot whaur the money had come fae. They waitit, but naebody came, sae they took a big cloot an left them in the bottom o the barra an pit a puckle strae on tap o't.

'We'll sait for a day tae see if anybody comes an if they speakaboot it I'll show them where it is an tell them I pit it there for safety.

They waited aa day but naebody came. That nicht they went tae bed and they were lyin. 'Hey, man,' she says, 'rise and look at the pot.'

'The pot's there,' he says.

'Jist rise and tak one look at it!'

'Awa!' he says. 'I'm mad wi you an your pot! God, hear my prayer! I wish ye'd never seen that pot! I hope someone taks that pot awa fae ye tae I get some peace!'

The next day when they got up, the pot wasnae tae be seen. It was away!

'There noo,' she says, 'I telt ye there was somebody knockin aboot this camp. Ma wee pot's away and I wadnae hae lost that pot for ony money!'

But they never saw that pot again. Next day they went awa doon the glen wi their wee barra an this cloot fu o gold sovereigns. Whatever happened tae them I dinnae ken, but I never met them since. I could dae wi meetin them tae get a shillin or twa off them!

One of the most important points of this story is that the travellers do not expect the gold sovereigns to solve all their problems. Certainly they will never want for the essentials of everyday life and that was enough for them. In fact they regarded the windfall as a potential problem for them. The traveller man's cry of, 'We're quoddit!' recognised the fact if they were found with the money it would be assumed that they had stolen it.

Therefore they hid it in their cart under the straw. Travellers do not flaunt their possessions, particularly money. They may take pride in the fact that they can go out every day and earn their living, but they also know there will be hard times and times of plenty. Like Willie, they try to take the rough with the smooth. They also, like Geordie MacPhee in Andrew Stewart's story, share whatever they have with their friends. So if Willie had met the couple in the story, he knew they would share their good luck with him.

Like everything else in Willie's life his belief in the super-natural must have changed as he went through the various stages of his long experience. No doubt as a young boy and man he was part of the old travellers' world and believed in haunted places, bodysnatchers and magical objects. As he grew up and became aware of other worlds around him he must have realised that intelligence and emotion were two different things. He developed the ability to use the beliefs that were still embedded in his community, and the human race in general, to add effect to stories. It was hard to tell where belief gave way to artistic purpose. In a way, this is a sign of a good storyteller. In Willie's case, I think the issue was blurred by the fact that he was a very spiritual man who tended to see the religious faith he had as part of, or akin to, his belief in ghosts and apparitions.

At the same time, it can be seen that magic and transfor-mation was essential to achieving all the turns and twists of the story. Storyteller Paraig MacNeil has told me of performing in a school with Willie at the Fair City Story Festival and telling a Gaelic story in English that had a lot of 'I will give you such-and-such if you will get the so-and-so for me' which really appealed to Willie. A year later he heard Willie tell the same story, having learned it from one hearing and it had the same storyline. I have two versions of 'Friday, Saturday' and 'Johnny

Pay Me', the former two recorded eighteen months apart and the latter two six months, and both have retained the same sequence. The supernatural element certainly complicates the story but the way Willie remembers the story bit by bit in a sequence helps to give it a framework.

Belief in the supernatural may be a survival from the days when many changes or events were unexpected and seemed arbitrary and inexplicable. The human mind always tries to make sense of life, and much that was explained by the supernatural in the past is better understood now, although many people may cling to old ways of thinking and have not the ability to leave the tramlines. In stories, this is exploited and 'a willing suspension of disbelief' is required to enjoy them. There are people who think TV is real, and that events and characters in soap operas are actual happpenings and people.

In stories some of the changes are symbolic, as when Jack in 'The Three Feathers' finds himself dressed like a prince, or Johnny in 'Johnny Pay Me' shows the strength of the lion, the agility of the salmon in the water and the speed in the air of the hawk. It is as if Willie uses the shape-shifting as a kind of graphic shorthand to illustrate how his character feels in terms of the quality he embodies. The beauty of oral tradition is that the story is told in the sound of words, has vivid visual imagery and does not necessaily involve belief. Supernatural motifs were invariably visual, like the road of enchantment, the brown hare, the piglets roasting on the fire, the ugly hag, the three hairs with extraordinary strength, the fantastic ritual of killing the giant whose heart was in an egg. This visualising of the motifs in the story is the best way of presenting it to a listening audience. A told story is always more alive than one that is read. If you compare oral and literary versions of folktales, you will find two different ways of telling them based on the ear and the eye.

7 The Perthshire Years

These began from the fact that Willie's father, Andrew MacPhee, and Alec Stewart's mother, Agnes MacPhee (Perthshire Nancy), who married Alec's father, the great piper John Stewart, were brother and sister. Alec and Willie became like brothers and for years used to go piping up the glens together. Willie's first wife was called Mary.

My late husband, Andrew, and I met Willie and his second wife, Bella, in the 1960s, in the Stewarts' house in Yeaman Street in Rattray. After that, we shared many a good night of song and story and the odd dram and many years of loyal friendship. Like everyone else, I loved Willie as a big man in every sense of the word, a person of great integrity and generosity of spirit, interested in everything that was going on in the world, very wise and perceptive, articulate and humorous. He was a fine storyteller, singer and piper, at all the ceilidhs in the Perth area and all over Scotland, and I was honoured that he contributed great, ancient folktale versions to my PhD project for Stirling University. I was fascinated by his ability to keep the structure and sequence of a complicated story in his head and re-tell it to suit particular audiences without altering its constant features or leaving out any of its essentials. His repertoire seemed endless and he carried the authority of a true tradition-bearer very lightly.

I was grateful to him for piping and singing regularly at ceilidhs I ran in Perth in the Windsor and the Tay Motel during the 1970s and '80s for the Traditional Music and Song Association (TMSA). He was also recorded by the School of Scottish Studies and became a founder member of the Scottish Storytelling Forum based at the Netherbow Arts Centre in Edinburgh. He was a familiar figure at their monthly Guid Crack Club, at their annual festival in the Netherbow and at other venues in and around Edinburgh. He was frequently invited to the School of Scottish Studies to take part in ceilidhs or talk to the students. He also visited and guested at traditional music festivals such as Blairgowrie, Kinross, Keith, Kirriemuir, Auchtermuchty and Newcastleton as well as Highland Games, particularly the Cowal Gathering.

After a restless period, Willie had eventually settled down with Bella, another cousin, whose husband, also a MacPhee, had been a sergeant in the army. He died after the Second World War, following a serious head injury received in an accident, while doing seasonal farm-work. Bella already had a family to her husband, including Isaac and Cathie, whom Willie brought up as his own. 'Willie brought me up from the age of seven,' Isaac told me, as noted earlier, 'I never knew any other father but him.' He had known Willie before his own father was killed. As Isaac was born in 1956, this dates Willie's new partnership from 1963. Cathie also makes the point that she has known Willie all her life and as far as she is concerned, he was the only father she could really remember.

Willie always enjoyed the conviviality and the singing and storytelling that used to happen round the campfire. 'It used tae be a great thing wi the travellers in the old times, when they had a few jars o whisky – this was their occupation, they wad hae telt ye, storytelling and singing tae wan anither. I learnt a few songs like that and I also learnt a guid few songs goin tae these ceilidhs and places [like folk clubs and TMSA events], hearin different singers, and hearin singin in a different wey fae the wey I sing. I more or less like a comedy song, wi a bit o life in it and I like Irish songs a lot.'

Johnny Jump Up

I'll tell you a story that happened to me. The day I went down to yawl by the sea. The day it was fine and the day it was warm. Says I, 'A cold pint wouldn't do me no harm.'

I went in and I called for a bottle of stout,
Says the barman, 'I'm sorry, all me beer is sold out!
Try whisky, O Paddy, ten year in the wood!'
Said I, 'I'll try cider, for I heard it is good!'

CHORUS: *O never, O never, O never again*
If I live to a hundred or a hundred and ten.
When I fell to the ground, sure, I couldn't get up
After drinking a quart of that Johnny Jump Up.

I went up to town, I made straight for the yard,
For I bumped into Mulligan, that big super Gard.
Says he, 'Come here tae me boy! Don't you know I'm the law?'
I up wi ma fist and I broke his old jaw!

He fell to the ground with his knees doubled up
Sure it wasn't that I hit him, it was Johnny Jump Up,
For the next one I met down at Youghal by the sea
Was a cripple on crutches and says he to me.

'I'm afraid for me life I'll be kilt by a car,
Wad ye help me across to the Railwayman's Bar?'
After drinking some quarts of that cider so sweet
He threw down his crutches and danced on his feet.

For I went up the lee-way some friends for to see
Sure they called it the madhouse, they called it Maree,
But when I got up there, sure, the truth I will tell
For they had the poor bugger locked up in a cell.

Says the barman, 'O Paddy say this if you can
'Round the rugged rocks the ragged rascal ran!''
Says he, 'I'm not crazy. Tell me I'm not mad.
It was only a sup of the bottle I had.'

A man died down town by the name of McNab
They washed him and laid him outside on a slab.
But after a moment his measures they did take
An his wife took him home for a bloody fine wake!

Now just about twelve the beer was gaun strong
And the corpse he sit up and says he with a song

'I can't get to heaven, they won't let me up,
Till I bring them a bottle of Johnny Jump Up.'

Another two Irish songs that Willie sang were 'The Maid of the
Sweet Brown Knowe' and 'The Lambs on the Green Hills'. The
first is a song of courtship, in which the young man is rich and
the maiden is poor. There is nothing unusual in that. But the
virtuous and proud young girl who rejects the extravagant rich
suitor is rejected in her turn and I have the feeling if Willie had
ever found himself in the same position, he would have done the
same. I have Willie's hornware dram cup, which I have had
circled with silver on which is inscribed his name, dates and the
words, 'His dram cup.' It is a testimony to the fact that he liked a
dram. The silversmith who made the silver mount expressed
great admiration for the beautiful workmanship in the cup,
which also shows respect for the man who drank from it.

The Maid of the Sweet Brown Knowe

Come all you lads and las-ses, come lis-ten to me a while. —— I'll
tell you of a verse or two that'll cause you for to smile, —— For it's
all a-bout a young man and a maid and I'm goin to tell you how —— The
fel-low fell a - cour-ting at the fit o the sweet brown knowe. ———

'O come on my pretty Catherine, come on along wi me,
For we'll both run off together and a-married we shall be.
We'll jyne wir hands with wedlock bands, I'm speakin til you now.
Sure I'll do my best, whatever I can, for the maid o the sweet
    brown knowe.'

'Look up in yonder green fields where my crops sae gently
    growe,
Look you down in yonder valley, my men are at the plough,
Look down in yonder valley where my men are at the plough,
They're at their daily labour for the maid of the sweet brown
    knowe.'

'Then if they're at their daily labour, then, kind sir, that is not
    for me.
I've heard of your behaviour. I've heard indeed,' said she.
'There is an inn where you call in, I've heard the people say,
That you rap and you call and you pay for all and come home at
    the break of day.'

'Then if I rap and I call and I pay for all, the money is all me
    own.
I will never spend your fortune dear for I hear you have none.
But you raved and you spoke and my poor heart's broke, as you
    spoke to me just now
But I'll leave you where I found you at the foot of the sweet
    brown knowe.'

'The Lambs on the Green Hills' is an Irish version of 'I Aince
Loed a Lass', another ballad of unrequited love. This version
particularly suited Willie's high, lyrical, expressive voice.

The Lambs on the Green Hills

The __ lambs on the green hills, they sport and they play. __ How

ma - ny straw - ber - ries grow in __ the salt sea? How __

ma - ny straw - ber - ries grow in the salt sea? __ How

ma - ny the ships sail the o - cean? ____

O the bride and bride's party to church they did go
And the bride she went foremost as part of the show
And I follaed after wi ma hairt fu o woe
To see my love wed to another.

O the first place I saw her was on the church stand
Gold rings on her fingers and her love by the hand
Said I, 'My wee lassie I'll still be your man,
Aye although you are wed to another!'

O the next place I saw her was on the way home
And I run before her not knowing where to roam
Says I, 'My wee lassie, I'll still be your man,
Although you are wed to another!'

'Stop, stop,' said the bridesman, 'tae I say one word.
Would you venture your life on the point of my sword?
But for courting so slowly you've lost that fair maid,
So begone for you'll never enjoy her!'

O dig me my grave, dig it long, dig it deep
And cover it over wi flowers sae sweet.
And I will lie down there to tak a lang sleep,
And that's the best way to forget her.

This next fragment must have been learned many years ago, and is all Willie could recall of the song. This demonstrates how dependent Willie was on his memory, which let him down rarely.

Mantle of Green

As I went out walkin one mornin in June
To view the fine spots and the meadows aroon
I spied a fair damsel she appeared like a queen
In her costly, fine robes and her mantle of green.

As I stood there before her I was caught by surprise
For I thought her an angel that fell from the skies.
Her eyes shone like diamonds and her cheek like the rose,
She was one of the fairest that Nature composed.

Said I, 'My pretty darling will you come wi me?
For we'll both join in wedlock and married we will be.

Willie also knew Scots songs and had a highly amusing version of a very popular song about a young girl courted by an old man, a situation that never seems to go out of date or lose its comic potential.

An Old Man Cam Coortin Me

An old man cam coor-tin me, Hey der-ry ho der-ry - An
old man cam coor-tin me, Hey der-ry dan. ____ An
old man cam coor-tin me, Fain wad he mair-ry me.
Maids when you're young ne-ver wad an old man!

When we gaed tae oor tea,
He started teasin me
When we gaed tae oor tea,
Hey derry dan.
When we gaed tae oor tea,
He started squeezin me,
Maids, when you're young, never wad an ould man!

When we lay in wir bed,
Hey derry, ho derry,
When we lay in wir bed
Hey derry dan.
When we lay in wir bed,
He lay as he was dead,
Maids, when you're young never wad an old man!

For he'd nae falooral
Nor yet a ding-dooral,
He had no falooral,
No, devil the one!
He had no falooral
Nor yet a ding-dooral,
Maids, when you're young never wad an old man!

When he was fast asleep
Oot o bed I did creep
When he was fast asleep,
Hey derry dan.
When he was fast asleep,
Out o bed I did creep,
Intae the airms o a handsome young man!

An he had a falooral
And yet a ding-dooral,
He had a falooral,
A hell of a one!
He had a falooral
Or yet a ding-dooral,
So, maids when you're young never wad an old man!

So there we played pitch and toss,
Hey derry, ho derry,
There we played pitch and toss,
All the night long.
There we played pitch and toss,
My maidenheid I lost!
Maids, when you're young never wad an old man!

Willie's songs were not all lighthearted, however, and he had a great version of 'Jamie Foyers', a Perthshire ballad about the death of a member of the Perthshire Militia in the Peninsular War. His tune is older than the one normally sung and has a haunting quality that suits the tragic story.

Jamie Foyers

To the Perthshire Militia to serve on the line
The brave Forty-Second all bound for to jyne,
To storm Brooks's Castle before the break o day,
Along with young Foyers to lead us the way.

But by climbin the ladder and scalin the wall
Wi a bullet from some French gun young Foyers did fall.
He leaned he's right arm upon he's left breast
And fell from the ladder putting off he's request.

'To you Robert Peerie who stands by campaign,
If goodness will send you to Scotland again,
You can tell my old mother, it's long may she murn,
That her son Jamie Foyers will never return.'

'But if I had one drink of Baker Brown's Well
My drouth it would swenchen and my thirst it would fell,
You can tell my old father if yet he's heart warms
That his son Jamie Foyers expired in your arms.'

They took for a windin sheet his bonnie tartan plaid
And in his grave poor Foyers was laid
Wi a heart fu o sorrow to cover him o'er
And young Jamie Foyers lay in his cold gore.
The war drums may drum and the meldrums [sic.] will rattle
Nae mair will this hero to row or to battle,
For he fell like a hero like a soldier so brave
And young Jamie Foyers lies in the cold grave.

The tune Willie uses is not the usual one sung today and is probably older. It is a variant of the first tune noted in the first volume of the *Greig-Duncan Folk Song Collection*. One of Robert Peerie or Pirie's descendants found an account of this incident among his grandfather's papers in the 1970s. Baker Brown's Well referred to a spring in Jamie's home village of Campsie. Willie admired tales of heroes, perhaps because his own family accorded him that status. He told us he was once 'the best man in five counties', in the sense of the strongest and fittest and most able to defend himself, which gave him a charisma that lasted him to the end of his days.

In the 1950s Willie was involved in a long-remembered fracas in Blairgowrie at the berry-time, when another traveller picked a fight with him in a pub and the resulting free-for-all was continued on the Stewarts' berryfield at the Cleaves, where they were all encamped. It is still known as the Battle of the Cleaves. This was followed by the Berryfields Court Case, in which Hamish Henderson tried to help the travellers by calling on the services of Lionel Daiches QC. Daiches got the charges against the Stewarts dismissed in twenty minutes by exposing the vagueness and inadequacy of the law.

You could see how travellers would enjoy this next tale around the campfire, or in their trailers, often camped in remote spots up lonely glens. It is a fact often forgotten, but which Willie reminded me of, that most travellers like privacy as much as anybody else. The type of story known as bodysnatcher stories, or, as the travellers called them, Burker stories, are not so entertaining, but quite frightening. My attention was drawn to them the night I had the Stewarts and Willie and other travellers ceilidhing in my house in 1974. They began to tell Burker stories and the atmosphere created was quite palpable. They not only told them as if they believed them, backing each other up, but also as if their fear was genuine. I was puzzled. Every one of them either attended the doctor or had been in and out of hospital, yet here they were shuddering and gripping hands as if they were all terrified of the medical profession! I began to realise what was going on. This was a ritual they had come to practise to allow them to face and live through their inner fear of outsiders. Every story had the same pattern. It depicted travellers in a lonely place living quietly and troubling no one, being set upon by men in tall black hats and long black coats, which the travellers called 'noddies', riding in black coaches with muffled wheels, drawn by horses with muffled hooves. The noddies tried to make off with them and sometimes succeeded, but in the end they escaped by the skin of their teeth.

In the early nineteenth century there was a real and justified fear throughout Scotland of 'the resurrection men'. Anatomy labs in universities could not legally procure bodies for dissection and so a criminal trade had flourished, culminating in the Burke and Hare case in Edinburgh in 1828. Burke and Hare took a shortcut in their methods: they plied their victims with drink and murdered them *before* they were buried, which saved all the nasty work of digging them up. It was only after their case that a law came into force that made it possible for the medical faculties to obtain bodies without breaking the law, so the ghastly trade dwindled and died. Fear of bodysnatchers became a thing of the past, but the travellers continued to tell Burker stories for the psychological purpose outlined. This insightful and wise use of storytelling was brillliantly illustrated to me the night this story was told. I also recorded John Stewart, Alec's brother, telling it and this is his version. But Willie also told us the story on another occasion, because Belle Reid had been *his* grandmother as well.

The Burkers and the Cuddy

Doctors at one time had to have bodies and these lonely tinks and people that stayed in woods, they were looked down on. Even when two or three went missing and ye went tae the police, they wouldnae bother. My mither was a wee lassie and there was an aunt o hers caaed the Big Dummy and an aunt o hers, big Belle Reid, six foot in her stocking feet, as mony o the auld tinkers could tell ye. My Uncle Rob was wi them tae. Noo the Big Dummy had tae be carried in a chair because she couldnae walk. An Rob had a Spanish cuddy, wi seggets on it, things hingin doon owre each side o it, and his tent sticks tied on and their blankets and tins and pans, hangin owre the cuddy's sides. They were gaun up tae this wood that they kent up a kin o cart track.

Rob pit up a bow tent and took the Big Dummy and let her

sit, gaed for watter and pit the kettle prop in. He hung the can on the fire an pit the tea and sugar and milk intae't, when the tea boiled and stirred it aa in the one thing, just the same as they would do in Australia, oot in the bush. They made a big can o tea and fried a bit ham, because bits o ham at that time any shop wad gie ye for nothin, for it wad go bad, because there were no freezers or anythin like that.

It wis getting kin o dark when Rob kennlet the fire and the donkey wis tied tae a tree. They'd a puckle hay for it, and a wee dog the size o a Yorkshire Terrier. Belle was standin at the fire and she looked away doon in the dark and she sees peeps o light comin up though the wood. She says, 'There a steejie bingin.'

'Where?' says Rob.

'Deek doon the road.'

They lookit and they could see the shape o a coach and a pair o horses. Noo whit wis a coach and a pair o horses daein up *that* way? Rob trampit oot the fire and he says, 'Gie me the wee dug.' And he took the wee dug, ma mither told us this for truth, and in case o the wee dug barkin, he took it and broke its neck and threw it owre amang the bushes. He got the Big Dummy on his back and got Belle and ma mither, a wee lassie aboot seven or eight years old, doon the road and awa through the wood tae where there wis a toll hoose. The man at this place knew Rob.

They ran and they chapped at the door o the lodge and the man cam oot and Rob says, 'Could you let us in for the night? Ony place you could let us in. They're up there wi the machine and we ken it's the doctors.'

'They're here every night,' the man says, 'searchin ma wee bits o ootbuildins. I'll let youse lie in the lobby. Have ye yer ain bedclothes?'

'We'd nae time tae tak bedclothes,' says Rob.

'Well,' he says, 'there a puckle jaickets tae keep ye warm. I've got a big dog there. It'll bark if they come.'

They were there for maybe half an oor and the coach come right doon and right up tae the toll hoose. An these men wi lum hats and tippets like Dr Crippen cam ridin up on horses. The man let his dug oot. Noo the coach had a dug and the twa dugs startit tae fight. The man at the toll hoose liftit his windae up and pit his gun up and he says, 'Call off your dug or I'll shoot it.'

They wadnae dae it and they were gaun tae come off and search the sheds. He says, 'Call off your dug or I'll shoot it. Now I'm givin ye warnin.'

But they wadnae and the man up wi his gun and shot the dug an they got intae the coach and went away.

Now in the mornin the man gien them some tea and he says, 'When ye go up tae your camp noo, I think ye'll be aa right. They'll no come back the day. But if I were you, I wadnae be here. I'd get up and get your bits o things and get out of it.'

So they traivelled back up the way they came doon and when they got up, the camp was in ribbons! Everythin was kickit aboot the place and the cuddy was tied up by the two hind legs tae a branch and its stomach ripped and its puddens amang its feet!

You ask big Willie MacPhee aboot that story! Every auld traveller in the North kens that story!

The late Hamish Henderson agreed with me that 'fear of outsiders' was very real among the travellers, with good reason. You have only to read reports of the arguments that took place in Perth and Kinross Council meetings when it was proposed to build the travellers' site at Doubledykes, and read in the local paper of the outrageous prejudices that were aired, that one realises the truth of this. I also remembered from my own training in counselling that inner fear is often dispelled by facing it, bringing out old suppressed memories and living through them to defuse their negative influence. This is what the travellers were doing by using Burker stories, which often have an unchanging basic structure. They begin with a family of travellers going about their business, camping in some lonely or isolated place, and being sought out by the Burkers, whom their imagination had depicted not as the bodysnatchers, but as the doctors themselves in long black coats and tall black hats. They would appear in a black coach with muffled wheels, drawn by black horses with muffled hooves and try to make off with some member or members of the family, who would either escape or return after almost being murdered. That night in 1974, I heard a Burker story that I have heard told both by John Stewart and by Willie MacPhee about their common ancestor, big Belle Reid. But Willie, of course, had experience of the Burkers himself, as he told us.

The Burkers at Crieff

This happened along time ago at Crieff, where I'd hawkit for a bit and I only had a pushbike and a tent. I cam tae Bridgend in Crieff in the back end o the year at tattie time. I put up ma tent and I went tae bed. Noo the tent wasnae very big and it wisnae broad enough for me tae lie across. I had tae lie wi ma feet tae the door. It wis one o these tent doors that ye lace up an put a pin in the bottom at the inside.

I'm lyin sleepin when I felt this thing at ma feet. I was tired: I'd been cyclin aa day and I dovered tae sleep again. This thing waukened me again and I says, 'Hoosh! Get away wi ye!' It went away but I didnae sleep this time, I kept awake. It came back an startit wi the door again. It was difficult tae open the door the way it was laced inside wi this pin. So I'm lyin wi ma feet tight up agen the door on the breadth o ma back. But finally the door was opened and it was dark so I couldnae see. Two hands came right down below the blankets and right roon ma two ankles. It must hae been a big man tae dae that! An he pulled me oot throu the door. An as he pulled me oot, some ither body was spreadin a sheet because ye could hear it faain on top o the leaves ootside and rustlin.

I says tae masel, 'That's no a dog!' I says, 'Hoosh! Get away wi ye!' and I pulled ma feet up and I went throu the side o the tent and scooted away throu the bushes. When I came oot, there were two or three o them and they just steppit back amang the bushes. They didnae try tae rush me. I went up the road tae some friends I had and I was maybe twenty minutes up there when a motor car came by and went back up tae the farm. When I came back, ma wee tent was ransacked and cowped and knockit doon an there was the track o the big car whaur it had turned just right aside where I was! When I ran oot that nicht, I'd never seen any car, for it was dark and I was goin too fast tae notice anything!

Any unrecognised car moving about on a country road or up a dark glen would arouse suspicion in lonely travellers because it meant strangers in the district. Willie makes use of this motif in his story of 'A Tinker in Ireland', where one of the adventures features a night-time hunt through fields with the terrified tinker trying to escape the car headlights of the faceless, nameless men who are after him. Also, farmers were often thought to be in league with the bodysnatchers, so a car on a farm road was doubly suspicious. Farmers were in some cases linked with magic and I have heard versions of a story that actually mention the farmer as having 'the black art'. Even in 'The Bailer' the farmer may have been responsible for Willie having a story to tell as a result of not being able to take his turn at the ceilidh.

At a Kinross Festival Jimmy Macgregor, a retired policeman who was also a singer and entertainer, remembers an incident, when a family concert was on in the town hall and the entrance area, which opened off the street, was full of artists waiting to come on stage and festival-goers who wanted to talk to them. Some of them had put their instruments on a table and one of the crowd, a traveller, as it happened, had 'borrowed' one of the accordions. The concert's co-ordinator had come out backstage and told the rabble to move, as they were making too much noise and it could be heard in the hall. The accordion disappeared with everyone else, but the 'borrower' was soon apprehended and locked up. At the same time, a woman's handbag went missing. Jimmy met Willie, who knew the man who had 'borrowed the accordion', and asked him if he thought the same man had also stolen the handbag. 'He might have,' Willie said, 'but I don't think so. Could I have a word with him?' Jimmy offered to accompany Willie to the police station where the desk sergeant let Jimmy take him to the cell. There ensued what Jimmie describes as 'the wildest interrogation that I've ever seen or heard'. Willie was going to use his authority to get the truth out of the man, come hell or high water. The man looked, Jimmy said, 'like a weasel caught in a headlight'. When Willie came out, he told Jimmy that the man had had a few drinks and had walked out with the accordion without meaning to steal it, but he had not taken the handbag.

Jimmy also recalls asking Willie to play his pipes to start the Saturday night concert at a TMSA Keith Festival. In this case, Jimmy was the concert compere and turned up early to see the hall. He found Willie and Bella among the people beginning to turn up outside and thought Willie might be taking part in the concert. But at that time, the TMSA had not realised that Willie was one of the tradition bearers they should be involving in their festivals. 'Naw, naw', said Willie. 'They wadnae ask *me*.' He was not at all bothered by this, but Jimmy thought *he* would ask him. 'Do you have the pipes with you?' Willie soon fetched them from his van and Jimmy told him, 'When the concert opens, I'll welcome the folk, and then I'll introduce you. When you hear your name, just come in the double doors at the back of the hall and march down the aisle playing. Then you can walk up and down in front of the stage.' Willie did that and created a great sensation, even though he was not in his Highland dress. He played a lively selection of tunes to open the concert. The audience was delighted and after he had marched out, Jimmy told them he was a piper of the travelling people, who had done so much to keep the tradition of song and music alive.

Willie was a great man for a ceilidh and often piped or told stories or sang at ceilidhs in my house. For example, when the Californians came for their annual visit under the leadership of Keith and Rusty McNeil from the University of California, Santa Cruz to do their 'Folklore Britain' course, Willie would welcome them with his pipes in the front garden. Then he would mesmerise them with stories in the course of the evening. These were memorable nights and the Americans soon learned to regard them as the highlight of their visit. At the TMSA ceilidhs in Perth, Willie would pipe, sing, tell stories, *cainntearachtd* and even play the Jew's harp or the moothie. There was one ceilidh in the Tay Motel where I did not expect to see him, as I had heard he had been involved in a car accident up north. But he turned up, with a gashed forehead and broken ribs, and performed, although it must have been agony for him.

When Doubledykes caravan site was finally set up for travellers at Inveralmond on the outskirts of Perth, after a long period of wrangling with the local council, Willie secured a stance there, as did other members of his family. With my husband, Andrew, I often visited the handsome trailer, with its pretty garden planted by Bella. It was a comfortable place to sit and share news with friends, drink tea or whisky and eat rolls, buns and cakes. The curtains and cushions were colourful and photographs and pictures covered the walls, along with ornaments and souvenirs. We listened to Willie's stories and sang songs or just gossiped. But Willie and Bella never ran down other people or expressed bitter feelings. Once, we visited them and Asian traders arrived on the scene. They had obviously called a couple of weeks before and had promised to return. It was fascinating to watch the interaction going on between two lots of people who had centuries of experience in trading and dealing. They played the game according to rules they both understood, unfailingly polite and friendly, but Willie and Bella were just as determined not to buy as their visitors were to sell them something. The unfortunate Asians had called previously when the children on the site were at school. Now it was the school holidays and the children were all there, crowding round, touching goods, asking questions and taking things to show their folks. The man in charge smiled endlessly, begging the children to bring things back, not to touch, but I feel he may have 'lost' one or two items. Willie and Bella shook their heads, claimed they had no money, that the 'nice warm cardigan' was the wrong size, when Willie surprised us all by buying a shirt. After the traders had replaced all their goods in the boot of their shiny big car, and driven away, Willie told us he had seen the same shirt 'in the town' at a dearer price.

Along with others on the site, Willie lost his trailer to the floods of January 1993. Willie and Bella lost all their possessions, apart from Willie's pipes that were rescued by some young lad diving in and pulling them out. They were Willie's most precious possession.

That same year Willie was still, in his eighties, a remarkably strong man, despite heart trouble, backache and cataracts in his eyes that put an end to his driving. We ceilidhed indoors at

Doubledykes, in Belle and Alec's house, at our house in Scone, at Duncan Williamson's house, at David Campbell's house in Dundas Street in Edinburgh, and at the School of Scottish Studies. Willie always played his pipes, sang, played moothie and did *canntaireachtd*. One year, Auchtermuchty Festival booked Willie as a storyteller, after I had pointed out that the storytelling competition was not supported enough because few people knew what was required. The festival booked singers, fiddlers and other musicians, but they had never booked a storyteller to be heard in the concerts and ceilidhs. Willie came on the Friday night and took part in the festival events, but on the Saturday he disappeared. He was nowhere to be found and the committee had no word of his leaving. It turned out as I suspected. He had left, because he felt it was his duty to attend the funeral of a relative.

A local farmer from Rosefield near Scone once contacted me 'to put me right about the travellers' on whose behalf I had been writing to the press, supporting their human rights to have a local site. He came to talk to me in Scone, and told me what a mess the travellers created in the lay-bys and how their dogs worried his sheep. I listened to all he had to say, then asked him if the travellers had not been doing seasonal work for him for years, shawing his neeps and lifting his tatties. He looked at me in amazement and said, 'Oh, but I'm no talkin aboot *oor* traivellers!' He spoke almost affectionately about the ones who came and worked for him, the Reids, the Townsleys and others, whose heather reenges, baskets and hornware he greatly valued. The late Betsy Whyte who had spent her childhood in Perthshire, confirmed to me that the farmers would employ local travellers, but looked askance at outsiders. Both the late Belle Stewart and Isaac MacPhee have described to me how travellers, 'follow the work' round the country throughout the year.

Of course one of the most important things in the traveller's life is what I call the ceilidh culture, which is part of the way in which family and social life operate among travellers and traditional music circles in Scotland. This period of Willie's life mirrored the earlier years which he had spent 'travelling through Scotland and Ireland' with his family, picking up stories and songs around the campfires. He now found a world in which songs, tunes and stories became highly regarded and where he could play his pipes and tell stories and sing songs in house ceilidhs and village halls and bars. Willie always opened the TMSA Ceilidhs I organised in Perth with set of tunes. When I say 'organised' I mean I booked the venue, sold the tickets and waited to see who came. There was no 'programme', like a concert, but everyone in turn was free to contribute something and in between these contributions, we danced, ate, drank, newsed and cracked. If I had a ceilidh in my house, I simply said there was a ceilidh night and people came or stayed away. There was nothing prescribed.

Willie did not share the outlook of many other travellers who had been influenced by folklorists, collectors and filmmakers – in other words people with their own agenda – into making romantic gimmicks of things like the Cant 'language' to create a romantic picture of 'traveller culture'. They present it as something separate from Scottish culture and tradition, even though history shows that to be nonsense. This has led even to travellers themselves and certainly many academics talking about 'traveller stories' and 'traveller songs'. As has been pointed out by many singers and storytellers and people who have known travellers, like the late Hamish Henderson, the rest of the Scots population, including both Scots and Gaels, owe a tremendous debt to the travelling people for keeping the ceilidh culture alive. They did this because of their partly imposed and partly chosen

social isolation and rejection of *scaldie* values. Our school system
has for too many generations left most of us deprived of our
languages, traditions and history. This lost ground cannot be
made up overnight but only gradually, in the wame way as
people like me, who lived throught the Second World War and
the Folk Revival, learned to value people democratically and
began to make the truth clear, helped to a huge extent by the
wisdom of people like Willie MacPhee. He was one of the
strongest links we have had with the culture we have neglected
and almost lost. His role in the Folk Revival in particular was the
right one: he was always there, a part of what was going on, and
did not involve himself in the commercial scene which
developed.

This commercial scene may have produced some dazzling star
performers, but a tradition is not carried on by 'big names' but
by a mass of people who love their songs and stories and music
and just want other people to enjoy them. The commercial scene
has brought some travellers under influences that have affected
their performance and given them ideas that, while they may
have created a market for them, have undermined their integrity.
The reason for this is that some folklorists and filmmakers,
driven by their own vision of what travellers are about, do not
know enough about them to realise that their intentions towards
them may be interpreted differently than they meant them to be.
This has definitely happened in the past, in connection with at
least one book, several films and a number of radio programmes.
In most cases the travellers have been unaware that they have
been misunderstood or misinterpreted. In others, they are aware
of this but are prepared to go along with this for reasons that
might surprise those responsible. Suffice to say that travellers do
not need to romanticise their past or present themselves as social
pariahs or tragic figures oppressed by unjust laws. They are

heroic, dramatic and fascinating people, for completely different reasons.

The best way of collecting stories and songs among travellers and learning from them is to ceilidh with them. This is not just my idea but is shared by many people and most of us learned this from the late, great Hamish Henderson. He spoke about being 'a participant observer' and that is how I look on myself. It has been my privilege to enter this world by virtue of my friendship with people like Willie and Bella and their family, and their cousins the Stewarts. I did not cynically set out to use these people, but only to share my knowledge of them with other people.

As a result of my including Willie in my PhD project for Stirling University under the supervision of David Buchan and then Emily Lyle, my thesis, field recording and video were lodged there and in the School of Scottish Studies. Willie's stories also appeared in my collection of folktales, *The King o the Black Art,* published by Aberdeen University Press in 1987, and his own account of his life and his songs was in *The Sang's the Thing,* published by Polygon in 1992. In both of these books I transcribed Willie's own recordings of these stories. Willie became a regular visitor to the Ethnology classes and student ceilidhs held in the School of Scottish Studies. He also was a founder member of the Scottish Storytelling Forum at the Netherbow, where Donald Smith invited him as a guest storyteller to the Scottish Storytelling Festival, and the Guid Crack Storytelling Club meeting on the last Friday of every month.

During this time, Isaac was a constant help and protector, then Cathy came to live there to care for him and Bella, a faithful and heroic daughter. He visited friends, and family, folk clubs and festivals all over Scotland. Andrew and I often visited them at

Doubledykes. He was also visited by collectors, students, journalists and makers of films. This continued until he was hardly able to leave his caravan. Louise Hay remembers one of those pre-Games gatherings in Inveraray, when he turned up and played to the company in the George Inn, whose noisy patrons fell quiet to hear an old man in his eighties play the pipes in public, perhaps for the last time. He was latterly often in Perth Royal Infirmary, where the medical staff loved him dearly, and it was from there that he was allowed home in November 2001, to familiar surroundings by the River Almond. But he had to go back to hospital. I visited him there and found it almost unbearable to see such a big strong man, a fine piper, storyteller and singer, reduced to a scrawny bag of bones that could not speak. Ironically, how much better he looked in his coffin, with his wonderful face with its handsome features, his tartans and his great leathery hands in repose.

The renowned folklorist Margaret Bennett was a close friend who visited him in hospital and described her visit in a journal she kept:

[He was] just a pale shadow of the strong sinewy man he once was . . . The day was humid and hot; he was eating an ice-lolly when I walked in – the nurse had given him it, as he was trying to keep cool. But he struggles for breath between bites . . . Now entirely without speech Willie can still express himself with eyes and hands . . . We arrived at a tranquil silence so, quietly, I spoke of Martyn, of how Willie was the first to tell him, 'These are piper's hands, laddie.' . . . At once his eyes danced and he fingered an invisible chanter, playing a tune, fingers birling and the rhythm steady . . . I told him I had been through Glencoe this summer and could never see it without seeing him . . . I could see him playing a precise rhythm and no doubt he heard every tune in his head. His mind still holds all his tunes and stories, all intact, but his speech is gone.

Willie MacPhee was buried in November 2001 in Gartocharn in West Dunbartonshire in a country graveyard, within sight of Loch Lomond. Everyone present felt that we had seen the end of an era, with the passing of the last of the tinsmiths, and that the world was a poorer place for losing him. There is no better way to understand the travellers' strong sense of family and kinship than to attend the funeral of a man like Willie MacPhee. My son Colin and I set out from Scone – my late husband Andrew did not feel up to going as he was not keeping well – but we felt that we had to go and pay our respects. All went well as we drove down to Doune, but after that we must have taken a wrong turning and got lost. We must have been driving all over the place and were sure we were going to miss the funeral, then suddenly we came round a corner and there was the little country church, with about a million travellers surrounding it. The minister was a tall genial man, who welcomed everyone warmly and conducted the service with dignity and sincerity. Then we all went out to oversee the burial and the minister and the beadle did not seem to mind the many feet that trampled over the rest of the churchyard. Beautiful wreaths lay round the grave, including one in the form of a stand of pipes, and the family pall-bearers laid the big coffin in the earth. A huge wave of emotion swept over us, and I was very aware of the feeling of togetherness that united us. It was one of those timeless moments that seem to allow a glimpse of the meaning of life. I lifted my eyes and saw that Willie's resting-place was within sight of Loch Lomond and all the natural loveliness of the countryside. He will sleep in peace there. As we made our way homewards we knew that he would live on in our hearts forever.

Lament for the Last of the Tinsmiths
(Tune: 'Johnny My Man'. Words: Sheila Douglas)

Dumbarton is mournin and Perthshire lamentin
The story is ended forever and ay
The dark glen nae mair will resound tae his pipin
The last o the tinsmiths lies cauld in the clay.

CHORUS: *O let us aye mind o the tales that he telt us*
The tunes that he played ne'er forgotten shall be
Aa the ninety-one years that the great hert was beatin
O the man caaed the Blacksmith, Big Willie MacPhee.

There was mony a ceilidh when his company cheered us
An mony a journey he made on the road,
Wi an ee for the beauty that rase aa aroon him
In the haunts o the wild deer, the hare an the toad.

He yince was the best man in all o five counties
As strang as an ox, wi nae fear in his hairt,
Wi the travellers' skills in the banes o his body,
An a mind fu o wisdom, a tongue fu o airt.

He gaed wi his pipes tae the Heilans an Islands,
Tae play for his livin by lochside an ben,
An he ne'er tuik a hoose but aye bade in a trailer
Whaur he fun aa the freedom nae scaldie can ken.

Nae mair he'll be seen at the gaitherin in Cowal
An the folk owre in Islay will luik for him lang.
Roon the warm bleezin ingle his face will be missin,
Whaur he used tae stap by for a crack and a sang.

Let's aa jyne oor voices in praise o Big Willie
For nae man was mair kindly nor kingly than he.
He's left us guid memories tae comfort oor sorrow
The last o the tinsmiths, Big Willie MacPhee.

BIRLINN LTD (incorporating John Donald and Polygon) is one of Scotland's leading publishers with over four hundred titles in print. Should you wish to be put on our catalogue mailing list **contact**:

Catalogue Request
Birlinn Ltd
West Newington House
10 Newington Road
Edinburgh EH9 1QS
Scotland, UK

Tel: + 44 (0) 131 668 4371
Fax: + 44 (0) 131 668 4466
e-mail: info@birlinn.co.uk

Postage and packing is free within the UK. For overseas orders, postage and packing (airmail) will be charged at 30% of the total order value.

For more information, or to order online, visit our website at **www.birlinn.co.uk**

Birlinn Limited

IMPRINTS: JOHN DONALD · POLYGON